THE COMPLETE GUIDE TO ATTENTION DEFICIT DISORDER IN ADULTS

BOB BRAY AND GEORGE BISSETT

ADHD Workbook Boxset

ISBN-13: 978-1-988152-06-6
Attention Deficit Disorder in Adults

ISBN-13: 978-1988152035

Attention Deficit Disorder in Adults Workbook

ISBN-13: 978-1988152042

The cartoons in this book are not intended to offend or minimalize the important issue that is Attention Deficit Disorder and Post Traumatic Stress Disorder. It is an interpretation from my own personal experiences.

"If we couldn't laugh, we would all go insane."

Robert Frost

Table of Contents

ATTENTION DEFICIT DISORDER IN ADULTS

BOB BRAY

INTRODUCTION

"They say I have ADD, They just don't understand…Oh look a squirrel."

I believe that there is a relationship between Attention Deficit Disorder/Attention Deficit Hyperactivity Disorder (ADD/ADHD), addiction, Post-Traumatic Stress Disorder (PTSD) and any stress-related problem that people can suffer from. I also personally see the relationships between these topics firsthand as I have been diagnosed with ADHD, and addiction. PTSD was my own diagnosis (psychologists missed it, but just for four years) as to what I suffered, saw, or felt, and I had suffered many stress related problems such as addiction, anger (uncontrollable), depression, anxiety, impulsivity, disorganization, procrastination, short attention span, and saying or doing stuff that seemed like a good idea at the time (but sometimes was not).

PTSD, by definition, can be a terrifying event that you can witness or experience and you may not be able to put it out of your mind. It is your definition (what you think it is). These are also ADD problems.

I am very grateful to my friend George Bissett, who helped me figure out what I had to do in order to control my emotions and behavior and learn how to calm down before I could actually figure out what I had to do to get better (Workshop). If we have problems or memories we cannot fix, we all too often tend to self-medicate with booze, drugs, sex, food, etc.

There are some ideas further into the book which can help you to better deal with your issues such as diet, supplements and exercise. There is also mention of foods or food products to avoid. I didn't explain that certain stimulants, such as coffee and energy drinks, are not good for us for if we are hyper-active, we will become more hyper. Many people believe hyper-active means we will be bouncing off walls, this is not totally true. We may be bouncing off the walls inside our heads. This also applies to many drugs both prescription and street drugs. I have heard many times that "marijuana helps me relax", maybe so, but it is addicting and, like many drugs, we become addicted. Now we have to deal with ADD and addictions.

I'd love to give you all the answers to curing ADD but I don't know if there is an actual cure. We teach methods to cope, manage and deal with ADD. ADD can be much more than a problem, it can be your greatest resource; it certainly became mine after I learned to use it to my advantage instead of a disadvantage. If you, or someone close to you, has ADD and has had it for twenty years, it will take some time to change. There is no magic pill where you can be instantly cured. If you are looking for ways to work with your kids, see my resources list or look up Barbara Coloroso, Kids are Worth It (several printings, it's timeless) and others. She is a genius in offering ways to work with kids which also works with adults. It helped me in helping raise my kids and I've used some principles of it for employees. This book and many others are part of what we need to help us educate ourselves into our problem and, if you got it, there is a good chance your kids will have it.

The depth of your disorder is somewhat of a difficult question and I believe we have to do a self examination to decide solutions as there are seven types of this and we can have many. The Amen Clinics offer some free testing and also more in depth testing and solutions. I offer methods of helping and controlling the thinking and behavior to a degree. If there is already a problem with a painful past, then I would suggest our workbook under the same name. It is a difficult path to walk, but you probably already understand or are used to a difficult life. The workbook will help you with coping, managing and dealing with your challenges. We also dedicate a part to creating a future plan if you could overcome these challenges to get you out of the rut you are in.

I am also grateful to Daniel Amen (a genius) of Amen Clinics, which is where I learned that ADD was my problem, not the addictions I had. The addictions came as a result of self-medicating in trying to cope with some of the symptoms of ADD and PTSD. At the clinic, I learned many ways of improving my brain through supplements, diet, and techniques to change.

I have taken, and continue to take, training in Neuro Linguistic Programming (NLP) as I had been big on reading about it approximately thirty years ago. I started to practice some of the skills and found that I could do amazing things in coaching people how to see their world differently. I took more programs on healing PTSD by another genius, Steve Andreas (one of the originators of NLP).

As I started to learn more about these three people and their different fields, I started to practice their beliefs, individually at first, and then began noticing that anybody I was working with seemed to have a common thread whether it was ADD, PTSD, Stress Problems, Addiction issues, etc., they all seemed to have ADD. I began using a combination of techniques from all three of these geniuses to help people recover from these various problems, and it has been working extremely well.

1

WHAT IS ADD?

"ADD people are high-energy and incredibly good brainstormers. They will often happily work 12 to 15 hours by choice. The business community should not fear ADD. Instead, they should see that they have a potential gold mine here." ~ Dr. Kathleen Nadeau, a psychologist who is ADD herself

I want to give you a little background on what ADD looks like in people, so you can better understand how this will impact people when life problems occur. Let's look at the simplistic model first. Daniel Amen first described someone showing some early signs that can alert us to future problems:

Short Attention Span is when we have problems in school or work when it is difficult to stay focused on instructions or what we have to do. If we miss part of the instruction, how on earth can we do the job or homework properly?

Distractibility is the notion that we can easily be taken off track to look around to see distractions or hear noises that are more stimulating than the topic in front of us. Some make jokes about squirrels, or others about bees and lots of them.

Disorganization is the state of your room, locker, desk, or your workspace. If it troubles others or you can't find something that you know is there, somewhere you might qualify for this.

Procrastination is when you put things off because you just don't feel like doing it at the time. It may be easy but boring, or it could be hard or maybe, you just don't feel like doing it right now. Something like taking out the garbage, I'm busy doing anything but that.

Saying or doing things without thinking them through. This is hard, but I have hurt a few people's feelings at times because what I thought was funny didn't seem to be from their perspective. I know I wouldn't like to admit I have done something stupid (is that lying?) and could lying fit here? If I had even stopped to think for just a second, I might not have done it.

These are all symptoms or early warning signs of ADD / ADHD, and if left untreated, or improperly treated, they could lead to more problems. Some also believe that ADD is a children's problem, and we outgrow it as adults, I didn't. ADD contributes to school problems and marital or relationship problems (some say about 50%). I know I failed at three, one living together and two marriages, before I realized I was the problem. It can also lead to workplace problems and many more areas. It's not just about misbehaving or wanting to cause problems, it's about some serious imbalances that cannot be controlled by the person.

The hyperactivity associated with ADD (ADHD) is sometimes missed as we expect these people to be very active and sometimes bouncing off the walls, and many times they do. But they may also be bouncing off the walls inside their heads… and we never see it, but we live it.

We can mistake signs of ADD for improper diets largely consisting of sugar or high starchy carbohydrates, which can create bizarre behavior in anyone. But in an ADD person, things can become greatly magnified - and you might see a crash afterwards or even sadness (depression), forget about trying to learn or perform a task. Poorly thought-out diets can accentuate these problems, while planned diets with protein and supplements can help sufferers to better control their little or big brains but they are easier on us. Later, I'll talk of foods that can help us to control thoughts and behavior, especially if we are ADD.

This might be an example of an ADHD kid. I was in grade one on my third day. I sat in the very front row. My teacher continually put her hands on my desk and would stand there lecturing us. I swear she spent more time there than at the chalkboard. We also had a dispute because I thought my name was Robert and put it on my papers as my name. She decided to challenge someone, so she

said, "I don't have a paper to give you, but there is one with Robert's name on it. I don't know who he is." I said that my name was Robert. She said, "No it's not, you are Bobby." I felt somewhat humiliated but I was only six and somewhat unimportant. The next day, I was at school a little early and smeared a whole bottle of glue on the front ledge of my desk. Sure enough, a short time later, she put her both her hands on my desk. Sure, I was punished but didn't feel that bad, and others laughed. The point is we are resourceful and can be creative when pushed, perhaps because our brains can be a little over active when we are motivated – or even during those times when we're not.

Another thing to keep in mind is that ADD can be caused by a head injury or a whiplash injury from vehicle accidents or extreme sports (soccer ball off the head, being tackled, puck to the head), or a fall off a bike or fence, etc. They all look similar or the same. If we look at the many athletes who are able to function well and play their sports very well due to their training and conditioning, we might wonder why some of them have been able to harness the power of an extremely fast (ADD) brain. Do some of these guys/girls have substance abuse, sex abuse, or family problems?

There have been many studies over the years – see the Archives of General Psychiatry – linking ADD / ADHD to addiction issues. Some might question whether ADD sufferers seek relief from depression, anxiety, inability to learn or complete tasks, or just not living up to parents' or schools' expectations. It is just a problem of not knowing how to cope with or manage this sort of an idea that we may start drinking or drugging at an early age to self-medicate. Some also suggest that these are only a graduation from video games, which have lost their ability to keep our attention any more, and like most addictions, we need something that offers a little more calmness. What a foolish idea, that of a violent game that calms down our brain or keeps our attention.

However, if we look at human lives in general, we will see that those problems are struggled with by many of us. I believe that we turn to substances or sex-related solutions as they provide some type of relief. It may be temporary, but it is still relief. Sometimes, the temporary relief might be taken too far and turn into full blown addiction, but we don't always think about the long term as many of us are not geared up to think beyond the stresses we are experiencing, and we lose track of where we are trying to go in life. Besides, it's just a little bit of relief and just for right now. These drugs and activities stimulate the reward center of the brain to release dopamine, bringing more temporary relief.

Another good source of a little dopamine is starting a fight with siblings, our kids, a spouse, or parents. Some may look at it as attention getting, but it may also be a source creating a confrontational or chaotic situation which may produce a little or a lot of dopamine to provide a naturally produced drug to help one cope with the problems occurring in one's head. Acting negatively is another form of gaining some stimulant which progresses into depression and also being oppositional. This is also seen in the workplace, just another coping device. No wonder ADD kids and addicts hang together; nobody else wants us. We can be negative together, not to just discuss the weather, but we can enjoy a nice little uplifting negative discussion by being critical of someone else or something they may have done.

The easy availability of video games, high impact TV shows, sports viewing and participation, when used obsessively, can result in our brains creating the chemicals we need to obtain relief. We claim that we just need our downtime, or a break from studying, but what we really need is our "fix" or we become grumpy or miserable – which is similar to a drug addict craving their drug (depression). Parents can certainly argue, "I need some peace and quiet and it's the only chance I get is when the kids are sitting quietly playing video games or watching Breaking Bad." The biggest problem is that once our pleasure center can no longer produce the natural chemicals we need to experience or enjoy life, we need a new source for pleasure.

Many of us didn't come with manuals or receive training or information from our parents or schools to help us cope with or manage our ADD /ADHD. So being the bright people we are, we look for ways to cope – and some of those ways prove to be damaging. Many of us had these problems and became parents ourselves. We then struggled throughout our lives with compensating behaviors and managed to survive somehow. So the questions arise. *Do we still have problems and what about our kids, because if we had it, they probably will as well? Does life or behavior change because we wish it to be?* We only have to look and see if there is conflict in our household or our lives. *Do you have road rage, old resentments, or even stuff a week old, anxiety when we worry about what is going to happen tomorrow, some days, you just want to curl up and stay in bed and not go to work (depression)? Need that one drink just to take the edge off?*

Many doctors tend to treat ADD with medications, and many of us tend to treat ADD with illegal drugs or other forms of relief replacements – such as booze, video games, aggressive sports, sex, porn, etc. What is the difference, as they all provide only temporary relief, but no cure – just possibly addiction? We don't learn how to cope this way, instead we just continue down a path towards addiction. Drugs in any form can provide a temporary platform to enable us to learn how to cope, manage, or deal with our problems, and then figure how to get off the substance before we become really hooked. But do we learn how to cope, manage, or deal with our ADD / ADHD? Apparently not.

Just a few words about porn. This is new modern multi-billion dollar business that is highly addicting as it produces a lot of stimulants within your brain to again help us cope with problems within our relationships, problems in the workplace, or in school. There are a lot of free sites which helps get you addicted, and you might buy a subscription which gets a lot more hardcore. This produces dopamine in your brain, which again creates a need for more and again dulls your brain to natural stimulation, so you seek more porn or stimulation to satisfy a need sexually, but this is arousal for the reason of porn not your mate. Some people may even develop a need to seek more and more porn. You don't even need to leave the house for this one, but it gets progressively stronger for a more powerful stimulant. Read up on addiction for this answer. How much work (homework) or family time will this cost in terms of productivity and dysfunctional relationships? Would you want your mate having relations with you after being aroused by someone else's pictures or videos? I guess that would depend on your values.

What are the long-term effects of untreated ADD (see seven types of ADD below) and addictive behavior? All are very similar in nature, as they both cause long-term brain damage, which further impairs our ability to learn, cope in the world, or even deal with or manage our problems. If ADD sufferers don't get help, they will find ways to cope, which may lead to serious problems and further impair their ability to learn, cope in the world, or even deal with or manage their problems. Our ADD brains also become targets for Alzheimer's.

There are seven types of ADD as defined by Daniel Amen in, "Healing ADD":

Type 1 - Classic ADD – Inattentive, distractible, disorganized, hyperactive, restless, and impulsive.

Type 2 – Inattentive ADD – Easily distracted with low attention span, but not hyperactive, instead appears sluggish or apathetic.

Type 3 – Over-focused ADD – Excessive worrying, argumentative, and compulsive: often gets locked in a spiral of negative thoughts.

Type 4 – Temporal Lobe ADD – Quick temper and rage, periods of panic and fear, mildly paranoid.

Type 5 - Limbic ADD – Moodiness, low energy. Socially isolated, chronic low-grade depression, and frequent feelings of hopelessness.

Type 6 - Ring of Fire ADD – Angry, aggressive, sensitive to noise, light, clothes and touch;

often inflexible, experiencing periods of mean unpredictable behavior, and grandiose thinking. Possibility of Bi-Polar Disorder.

Type 7 – Anxious ADD – Anxious, tense, nervous, predicts the worst, gets anxious with timed tests, social anxiety, and often has physical stress symptoms such as headaches and gastrointestinal symptoms, and conflict avoidance.

Unfortunately, many doctors treat ADD as though it only needs Ritalin or Concerta, and one of these symptoms may respond to this type of blanket drug coverage, but with more than one type of ADD involved other problems may arise which can be in direct conflict with trying to use blanket types of coverage. That could be like trying to treat a headache by shining your shoes, some could say, it might work. Also, sometimes a diagnosis such as Bi-Polar arises within the ADD family, which requires a different treatment.

It has been said that ADD is misdiagnosed by General Practitioner doctors six out of ten times. I needed to do something more to help my son with ADD, and we decided to go to the Amen Clinics (http://www.amenclinics.com/) in the U.S. We needed a referral from our doctor. The doctor provided it, but said that my son just needed to work harder even though he had been clinically tested and diagnosed as having ADD. The doctor also provided a prescription for Ritalin. My son went to summer school throughout high school because he struggled so much with ADD issues. Apparently, I didn't have it, as it was only a self-diagnosis up until I went to the clinic.

Here is what it looked like to me:

During the cadet program run as an after dinner program, as well as some of the kids groups I would work with at times, I found many kids from differing age level have an inability to pay attention or behave in an environment conducive to learning or staying out of trouble. This was true whether for a church program or a structured cadet program. At times, questioning revealed a lack of dinner or sometimes cereal which was sugar based, or many times pasta without meat or protein. This would be made obvious through the evening by poor behavior, no focus, or kids just doing what they wanted. Timeouts or removal from classes provided no change.

During my tenure in the cadet program (cadets are 12-18 years), I began suggesting to kids to eat and if there was no food available at home to eat peanut butter (protein), preferably with a banana or fruit (complex carbohydrates) but not white bread (carbohydrates) which are part of the starches which turn to sugar when ingested and affect behavior in a bad way. Many families also provide lots of pasta from a box which may fill up the kids, but provide unwelcome behavioral problems. If speaking to parents, I might be reminded that what was fed to their kids was none of my business. I stuck to it trying to influence the kids and what they ate. This wasn't working twenty percent of the time. So I adapted and brought almonds, and began picking out kids whom I noticed were fidgety on arrival, I would provide about eight to ten almonds to each of these kids whom I would question about eating or eating nothing, or pasta or pasta from a box. All took the almonds and ate them, some at times grumbled and the odd discussion ensued, but it made a difference. I would also pay attention during the beginning, as some would originally pass the first scrutiny, but would have challenges focusing or paying attention in classes. My first solution was almonds and given time, twenty minutes to half an hour, this solution seemed to work. The bigger challenge was always the kids who had pasta or toast with butter or margarine, hamburgers, and french fries, who were already bouncing off the walls. The carbohydrates are easily ingested and convert to sugar in the body, and now you have more problems. Some of the bigger challenges were the kids who were taking Ritalin or Concerta or Prozac. These kids appeared like zombies or even sometimes uncontrollable, which may sometimes reflect the prescribing of the wrong medications.

2

WHERE IS THE LINK TO PTSD, ETC?

"There are many positives with ADD, including a surplus of ideas, creativity, excitement, and interest which accompany this kind of mind." ~ Sari Solden.

Let's look at the world today, and see what's going on as far as people getting into trouble. Bringing it closer to home, ever seen road rage, drinking or drugging, or family problems?

These problems may arise from simple ADD which has been ignored as a problem, or when we haven't been aware that we had such a problem and just learned how to cope by funneling our strengths into sports or hobbies and not doing great in school. We showed the world that we were good at stuff too. Some of us didn't have these qualities, so we learned to cope by drinking or drugging and sort of kept those habits all our lives. Maybe that stuff didn't work all of our lives, but it must have worked at least at one time for us to keep doing it all our lives. Some of us were able to function well at work, as we could become workaholics and devote ourselves to work. That way, we could minimize our time spent with friends and family. We were just too busy. I am a good family man as I am out there working to support you guys.

We suffer most of our lives with depression and anxiety, and inevitably learn poor coping skills at early ages. Unfortunately, due to these coping skills, we become somewhat emotionally stuck at whatever age we adapt to these addictive behaviors. I also know people who have begun drinking as young as eight years old, but who were raised in perfectly normal homes. If any of us were abused in some form or another, whether at home or school by parents, siblings, school mates, or teachers, we were unable to cope with the emotional effects of this abuse, and we became stuck. If the magnitude of these incidents becomes something that we cannot cope with or endure, we can suffer Post Traumatic Stress Disorder. The way I have found this to be significant is that at this point many incidents which happen to us from this date forward become somewhat stacked on top of the last incident. If we were unable to deal with the last incident, we will be unlikely to deal with the next one or any of the following incidents. We have become emotionally stuck at the point of the very first incident in our lives. Now what happens is these incidents continue to stack on top of the last one and become inter-twined with each other. The difficulty becomes when at some point during our life we begin to bury any of these or many of these incidents, especially if they were particularly horrible. Our behavior becomes sort of crazy without anyone being able to diagnose, let alone correct, the problems. This is a good time to increase your meds to control your symptoms, because who knows what the problem is now?

Many of us ADDers get depression with our ADD problem. We might also get bi-polar disorder as well. I believe the sadness comes from our inability to let go of our old painful memories. It's some of the learned things that we can cling to. I actually believe that we have trouble learning sometimes because our brain is quite occupied remembering these painful vivid memories which others might use to learn important things. These memories have been integrated into our brains because they are visual and colorful, we hear all the conversations whether screaming or threatening, the kinesthetic part especially if we are physically or sexually abused. If you pee your pants, you have a total experience that will be imbedded into your memory forever.

Because we are small, and mostly cannot fight back for fear of reprisal, our only payback might be the ability to get even by holding a grudge sometimes long after this villain has died or even visualizing some form of revenge. We are small, but we can catch on to things such as payback and keep it internal. So we did learn something: how to hang onto old memories and revenge. Unfortunately, we don't get to carry out that revenge part very often and live in frustration because of unfulfilled resentments. The very unfortunate part of this depression thing is that sometimes we can have so much of it and it can linger so long and at times so deeply that we aren't even aware of it that we might take our own lives.

You watch that side and I'll watch this side. Wake me if someone comes.

So let's add some counseling onto this. Now we have to live this over and over until the counselor believes that we have become conditioned to finally accepting this hurt because it doesn't bother us anymore. That has to be the biggest crock of shit I have ever heard of. I lived this luckily for only four years after the start of counseling, and the many years previous to counseling. But I know of people who have been going to counseling forever, and still feel the pain over and over. The good news is that even if you are in recovery program such as AA, counselors or psychiatrists can arrange a prescription for you for something to reduce depression or anxiety. When I was in counseling and attending AA at this counselor's suggestion, I was offered anti-depressants. I am just guessing these types of medications are not addicting or mood modifiers which interfere with your recovery. Maybe you will only get placebos, and struggle through like the rest of us trying to be free of addiction and dependency, but it is not likely.

A lot of people who suffer from some of the effects of ADD are drawn to types of employment where they can get some of the natural types of highs to make their brains feel better and have appropriately exciting employment. What I am saying is that we seek or we are predisposed to these types of employment, these are life and death decisions, it doesn't get much better than this, does it?

One of the challenges of these careers is we have to learn how to react to different scenarios with appropriate responses. We spend much time being indoctrinated in this new and different profession. We learn how to wear a uniform, develop a fitness program to change your body shape, change your hairdo, or learn how to be a soldier (discipline, history, teamwork, your buddy is everything). How to shoot at a target that pops up without discerning friend from foe. Some might call this hyper-vigilance training other might call it, learn how to have anxiety. Similar to police training except police are trained to pause before shooting the pop up target in case it is the woman carrying a child. When I went through police college, I had a problem shooting all pop ups as I was trained to react quicker without thinking. Still the police training was reactive in the sense of all calls you attend to are going to require a reactive response from you. Would this training increase your level of hyper-vigilance or again anxiety training? So

when we leave these professions, what happens to our hyper-vigilance training, do we forget or take our training with us as no one un-trains us? Some might liken this to brainwashing.

At times, we see veterans of the military, police, nurses, or other first responders who have seen or been involved in a particular gruesome or catastrophic event become unable to shake off this last scenario from their mind or memory. I would hazard a guess that this is when they have reached their breaking point, they have become overloaded with so much terrible memories over the years, and this has become the push over the edge. We also have to keep in mind the subculture involved which doesn't allow for these professionals to show weakness anywhere near their peers.

I see the parallels with people with addiction; they have become overloaded at some point and resorted to drinking, drugging, etc. However, I have come to the conclusion that their experiences have become intertwined together and manifest as depression and anxiety plus whatever was there before. The problem with soldiers and police is that their professions have made them hyper-vigilant in order to survive, and going back to normal life has left them with extreme anxiety.

Because this sounds so simple, let's add some other problems which commonly appear. Many times, I have seen people without goals. For them, it has become a question of survival just to get through the day. They have no idea what their future looks like, not even tomorrow. This makes them predisposed to not really caring about what they do in various circumstances.

If there is no future, it's all about today, getting through the now, and staying straight right now. How on earth can you ever get better unless you focus on how good tomorrow could be if you got better?

Not done, we also have to look at what this kind of lack of future will do to your values. We live in a state of paranoia (extreme anxiety), and we are trying to exist, we are self-medicating probably on top of whatever our doctor gives us for stress and now we are having some new problems from meds conflicting with booze or recreational drugs. Funny how they don't mix and cause more twisted thinking. But we don't get it; we are still just trying to survive. Who can possibly consider values such as fidelity when you are half stoned, let's throw sex into the mix, who knew this also offers a soothing effect and if you are a little crazier, one might even think this is a little bit of intimacy that I would like because I got screwed up as a kid and don't know intimacy? So a good one to accompany fidelity is lying, because your spouse isn't going to appreciate the truth in this. At the same time, you also lied to your kids by spending their time with another woman. Some of your friends may be real buddies in your mind and may be great in your workplace, but will they pass the test as upstanding citizens? I was a policeman for several years, and my ex-wife used to say if she were in trouble, she would not call the police, they might be worse than the criminal trying to victimize her. I wonder if she wondered if they were upstanding citizens? She was also an ER nurse, and she would see them first hand in work situations, which at times wasn't pleasant. This could get to be a long discussion, but I think that you are getting the idea of how values can change after we get overloaded with a problem spouse (not her but me). When you are fighting for survival that is first and foremost in your brain, and it is hard to come back to normal. We like adrenalin and replacements for it. Whether you are a street cop or soldier, how many non-hostiles do you get to deal with in a day, or how many with values intact? Whether on a mission or handing out a speeding ticket, how many people are happy to see you? Simple questions like what does my life mean and why am I here are not relevant at this time.

I want to make another point about the use of any form of drugs, alcohol, or whatever method of mind altering a person may use (sex, drugs, and rock and roll). A few of these may even be considered recreation, and some even non-addicting. It has been said that a simple narcotic such as marijuana is not addicting (wake up, it's a narcotic). If you give this to a person who has addictive or obsessive behavior and it works to alter their mood, guess what, they will keep using it. If you have to use something to modify your mood or escape emotional pain, you probably aren't satisfied with your life the way it is now. Now if you get grumpy (depressed) when you stop, there may be a problem. Same as any other drug or booze. What the heck, another illusion about passing some time shattered. Here in Canada, our federal leader of the opposition wants to legalize the use of marijuana as though it is not a narcotic that is highly addicting. We don't have enough problems now. I guess, he never heard it is a gateway drug. Unlike the rest of us who maybe prone to addiction, he is not. Some of us would be considered in denial if we couldn't stop using but a politician would never deny anything.

Many of these mood modifiers are also central nervous system depressants (alcohol for sure), which means that it lowers your inhibitions (values) and your values will change permanently over time. You might be willing to do something you might otherwise not do, maybe reluctantly at first, and then it becomes easier. Like if you don't use cocaine, you might be a little less critical of someone who uses it if you are drunk or high. This becomes a slippery slope, because if you think you are having fun stepping outside your normal boundaries, it will be fun but you have now lessened your commitment to the values you may have been raised with to fit into normal society. If you come from a screwed up family to begin with, you are going to need a little more of what anybody else might need. I wonder if watching pornography several hours a week or more will affect my values? Many people would argue that seeing women or men in a continual sexual role may lead to a misogynist (mistrust) type of belief about them.

The order in which these events can occur certainly change. I was working with a policeman who had been in an ambush situation, and felt that the situation had given him PTSD. He was on some meds for depression and anxiety, and couldn't sleep. We were able to determine that although this was stressful, this was not the cause of his PTSD. We looked at an ex-wife who was unfaithful and used drugs and wasn't a great mother for their kids. This was stressful, but was not the problem. He was obsessed about repairing the situation, and repairing her problems. We looked at another ex-wife, similar problems, but not the answer. We looked at several issues during his work life, teen years, and childhood. The issues were many, and certainly causes of depression and anxiety. He suffered abandonment issues at about two years of age, bullying in school because of weight issues, and friendships going bad. Basically a horrible past, but no real root cause. As we kept going through these issues, we determined that these problems were the cause of his depression and anxiety, and we were able to release all of these emotional stuck points from his memories. It was only under hypnosis that I was able to find an incident that occurred when he was nine years of age. He was abused, and subjected to some horrific trauma that he had completely blocked out of his mind. This was the release point of PTSD, but had also been the stuck point and everything afterwards stacked on top of it. He didn't have coping skills to get past this point due to the early events of his life. He no longer uses any meds, and has forgiven both ex-wives and the parties involved in his past. He carried this burden for twenty-two years without knowing or understanding it. He appears well adjusted now. He had been tested by another agency and found to be ADHD, a variety of types, with co-dependency and control issues. He was devastated by the revelation of ADD, but later came to realize the benefits of it. Co-dependency and control issues also needed to be sorted out.

I was at a hockey tournament when I was asked to meet with one of the players who had broken down in tears (someone recognized me for what I do). I was able to determine that the player had lost an addicted sibling to suicide and was unable to let go of the whole scenario in his mind. I was able to help this person to calm down for the time being, and be taught a quickly engaging relaxation technique. Sometime later at the office, I was able to provide some tools for coping with anxiety and depression and turn the suicide into an acceptable normal grief situation. There were also some issues of co-dependency and control issues with the family. There was ADD of different types involved here.

I worked with a man who had some stress issues, but wouldn't tell prior to us meeting. When he arrived at the office, he stayed outside and almost didn't come in. He also wanted to change his mind about coming the day before. He had depression, anxiety, and marital problems in the past. We were able to resolve these problems. He finally told me that a priest had sexually abused him fifty years ago. The priest had used many means to keep control over this boy. He had been fourteen at the time. He had said that he was a wreck, and he didn't know if he could tell anyone at the time, as he was led to assume that no one would believe him anyway. And whatever other forms of coercion were used on him. This abuse had lasted for some time, and the results were feelings of guilt, depression, shame, fear of this being held against him, fear of intimacy, and fear of being touched by his first wife. He was the victim, but felt that he was some sort of participant even though he had ended the relationship. He had lived his life in these conditions, but the memories had only started coming back in the last three or four years, this was PTSD caused over a long period of time, which caused problems throughout life, but the incident stayed hidden. Symptoms of ADD appeared in school but it was hard to determine when it started, as his childhood was pretty vague (blocked out by PTSD). He also showed signs of co-dependency.

My story is similar, with a painful past, but when diagnosed with ADD at a specialist clinic (Amen Clinics) in the U.S.A., I initially thought that was my problem and that I was making progress, but the counselor took holidays. I ended up seeing an alcoholism counselor who convinced me I was an alcoholic because I had all the symptoms of an alcoholic. Sure, I had been a drinker, but not a serious one, for about thirty years. I learned that drinking had helped my problem; it had been my solution long ago. I had been practicing a new obsessive behavior for a few years, work. I got involved with Alcoholics Anonymous (AA), but I wanted to get better. I didn't want to be an alcoholic forever. I have always had goals. I wanted to get better, and not have signs of a precarious type of sobriety with control and codependency issues. Maybe sobriety is precarious, and I'll always have the ability to make the decision of whether I want to have a drink or not but I want the choice, and also not to live in fear that I may drink again.

If you put a bunch of alcoholics in a room, you would find that they have very similar problems such as being grumpy (depression at times), resentments, anger, anxiety, brain races, short attention span (doesn't listen or pay attention), holding grudges sometimes for years, negative thoughts, poor control over money, procrastinating, many are disorganized, forgetting important dates such as birthdays, problems in school, etc. If you put a bunch of ADD people or kids in a room, you might find very similar problems. Look at the list of ADD types back near the beginning of this book, and you might be surprised. Why do drunks hang around together?

Probably the same reason that ADD kids do in school, they finally found a place where they fit in. They also learn that there are ways to cope such as arcades, booze, and drugs. The difference is that we may be born with ADD but not with control and co-dependency. We learn these.

The more that I went to counseling, the more bitter I seemed to get after reliving some of my childhood experiences over and over and doing workbooks. I got to relive the pain I experienced many times over. Was I getting better? Would you?

"Sometimes, if the experience is very traumatic and a person becomes amnesiac, she falls into the hands of a therapist who insists she should remember every detail. This is nonsense: people's unconscious minds are very protective; sometimes they make us amnesiac for a very good reason. The events that happened are just too terrible to have to recall." Richard Bandler's Guide to Trans-Formation Page 98. Richard is a co-founder of Neuro Linguistic Programming, which has changed the way to help people actually recover from serious painful memories, and behaviors which can arise from them.

My friend, George, hooked me up with someone who showed me how to eliminate these painful childhood memories from my life, how to focus on my future, and how to begin rebuilding and redeveloping my self-esteem. I did this for about nine months, and George taught me through one of his workshops how to change my moods immediately from anxious, depressed, and angry (road rage) to calm. Now I have shifted into high gear, and began correcting different types of behavior as I became aware of them. I like to think that GOD gave me a brain to use to fix myself and not to bother him every four minutes because I can't make it through traffic. He has got bigger problems in the world than trying to help me stop being annoyed by traffic. If I can calm down, I can use the full capacity of my brain to help me resolve my issues instead of just a portion of it when I am stressed. My method is to practice changing your mood often enough and it will become a habit, which will start to kick in automatically.

I don't drink at all anymore, as I don't want to. I learned how to have fun without it. I still go out with other friends who drink, but after I hear the same joke twice from the same person, it's time to go. There has to be more than that for me. I am motivated by goals and results of what I want. I like my life and the way it is, and I want to keep it.

Some say when you write a book you have artistic license. So, here goes, something I have been noticing about most of the people I have been seeing is that many have auto immune problems such as Colitis, Crone's or Irritable Bowel Syndromes, Ulcers, and other stomach disorders. I request medical information (prescription and recreational drugs usage), and family history when I start with a new client. It gives me a thorough picture of the person that I am looking at or working with. I have heard at times that these problems are stress-related diseases, but I'll leave that for doctors to diagnose. I also have colitis, but it is well managed more so since I have been able to turn my life around. I'm just saying, maybe this is something to consider. I have heard such gossip that there is also a link with heart attacks. The scary one is the one I heard about Alzheimer's somehow finding us ADD people and targeting us because our brains are already at risk or diminished from suffering much of our life with untreated depression, anxiety, or substance abuse. I am scared for the rednecks who keep pounding booze and drugs back until the bitter end, will they get better?

Here is where I take a little more of this artistic license. From what I know of myself and my struggles with life and the people I have met in policing or soldiering, and the many hundreds of kids that I have worked with over the years, I have seen many similar patterns. If you have ADD and you don't do anything about it, you become a target for stress-related problems including PTSD and, later in life, Alzheimer's, plus many will struggle with life.

3

THE PEOPLE WE ARE DRAWN TOWARDS

"I prefer to distinguish ADD as attention abundance disorder. Everything is just so interesting . . . remarkably at the same time." ~ Frank Coppola

Here is a big shock to our system, who do we hang around with? People who are very much like us. I never much went for rocket scientists or astronauts or even football or hockey players. I like what they do, but they have never invited me into their inner circles. We hang around people much like ourselves. If you are a welder, you might hang with other welders, and it is the same with electricians. If you are a drunk and hang around bars, who are you likely to meet there? If you are a cop, most of your buddies will be cops, if you are an ex-cop then your buddies will be ex-cops, they don't generally mix socially. When I left (honorably), they forgot me quickly. Take a look, who are your friends and what do they do or where did you meet them and what do you do together?

Unfortunately, we can get into these kinds of cliques which sit around and criticize what agencies are doing or not doing for us, how bad is the weather or football or hockey teams. Getting together with like-minded people can be enjoyable, and we have lots to talk about, but where will this take us? If you are going nowhere, then you are there. Venturing your opinion as to how to fix your world or the rest of it or your buddy falls on deaf ears for the most part. How many people actually take advice from others? If you are letting other people hold you back, you may have forgotten the first rule of leadership. It's like the airplane briefing. If the mask drops down, put your mask on first, and then help the other person. If you run out of oxygen while trying to help someone else, then you are both screwed. Get yourself together first, then you might be of some value to yourself and others.

I understand the term co-dependency and the implications, but what the heck does it mean? I do find a lot of co-dependency issues as well, whether the person is co-dependent or the controlling person, drinker or drug addict, this is another problem which requires a change in the way we think. Many people consider this a simple problem, but when we take a deeper look, we see that this is a form of addictive behavior as well. This one takes us back as far as we remember and further. I see that the start is when we are being raised, and it is fine when we are small and need to be instructed on most everything. But as we grow and tendencies for parents to continue telling us what to do and how to do it and when we don't do it the exact way we are told, we are now bombarded with dramatic corrections, emotional or physical abuse, and someone else may finish the task as we are not capable. We walk away further damaged by the insecurity of being unable to complete a task. One only has to take a few emotional hits like this as a kid to damage our self-esteem for later in life. As a result of role models such as this in our life, guess how we learn to act, as we get older? We can be helpless and always need someone similar to this type of parent forever, and we get to become this type of parent perpetuating this cycle on our children. The beauty of co-dependence is that we usually follow our parents, and co-dependents work in pairs. One is co-dependent, and the other is the one who abuses substances. From this, we learn the behaviors, and they usually follow sexual orientation, boys follow dads, and girls follow moms. This rule is not cast in stone, but it has a good chance of survival.

I believe that many of us come from similar types of situations, whether family types of dependency or misunderstood school or playground situations. Many times, we grow and learn to adapt, but we at times are seen as outcasts as we don't always fit in. Various schools of thought exist about it once we start into puberty. There are the cool kids who seem to be on a different plain comprised of jocks and cheerleaders. Some of these seem to be airheads and some may even have ADD or ADD brought on by blows to the head through sports, but they are readily accepted, for that is what we do in our culture. We like success at early ages and relish in it. The studious kids are sort of outcasts, except the ones who are able to excel at school and sports. The middle of the road kids who are neither cool nor outcasts seem to have their own clique. The ones who don't fit at all are the ones who don't fit anywhere. They have become outcasts because many of them struggle with school, and relationships with others, and more or less keep to themselves. Things are probably better today than yesterday. Yesterday, the teachers made it a point to correct you publicly in front of classmates, which actually made you feel stupid and, of course, the other kids would figure that out and some may have begun to tease or torment you, all in good natured fun, especially from the good natured jocks and cheerleaders who were so superior, and you needed to know that also in front of others. Today, if the teacher spends a lot of time with you trying to help you through the challenges of struggling with learning, I am sure the others don't notice and torment other kids nowadays. This is always the special education kids, which are always treated normally by everyone. The problem becomes that the kids who struggle always seem to know who the others are that struggle. Somehow, they drift together and try to keep a low profile and hang around. This group can comprise all kids who struggle. They have sort of given up trying to fit in, and become somewhat rebellious. They don't do their homework or participate in sports. Some become discipline problems like exhibiting oppositional behavior, they might have smoking issues and just not cigarettes, maybe drink when opportunities present, maybe become gothic dressers. The similarity is that they find they have much in common. They already have the stigma of not fitting in, and they may have issues at home as they have been raised in chemically abusive environment, or suffered abuse of one form or another. It's almost as though they speak the same language, they have so many similar problems, and they relate very well. Many of these kids will do anything to fit in somewhere, and here is the link up. They quickly learn coping skills to better handle their misunderstood world such as drugs, booze, and sex, or stealing for the extra dopamine high. Nobody seems to care; they are left to cope and human nature takes over, and cope they do.

The next phase of this story takes us to high school which many ADD kids (recall I mentioned the relationship between addiction and ADD) drop out of, fewer also stay but struggle as prescription drugs do work sometimes on some. We start at mate selection on a more serious note, but guess what sort of people are drawn together, the ones we can relate to and guess what coping skills they have to help them through life? Unfortunately, with or without high school, will these guys get the best jobs? The process is more set in stone at this point, the uneducated stick together, the ones with drug or alcohol issues stick together, and these are still usually the same groups. Unfortunately, whether a baby occurs or not, the relationship is doomed by about a fifty percent margin of failure. Life just continues as before, drinkers and those who believe that if I could just get my sweetie to stop drinking, we could be happy. The battered wife whose spouse probably drinks and beats her says the same. If only I could be a better wife, he might stop beating me. We bring our baggage to these relationships, it's whatever we saw our parents doing, and we will probably do the same. We just put on a good show at the beginning, and impress those who don't really know us and then the Jekyll and Hyde story becomes apparent. Can't hold a job or relationship, it started in our minds long before this, we saw and learned, and if we had untreated ADD we were so screwed.

Here is an example. I know a kid who has his own bedroom and bathroom in his house.

One day he phoned his mom and said, he was having some friends over after school. Would she tidy up his room and clean his bathroom, as there were some poop stains in his toilet. I guess he knew about them but did nothing. She did this, as they were both concerned as to what people might think or worse, say something to other people. If this were the only issue, maybe we could understand, but do you really think so?

It is great to be helpful, but has this seventeen year old got coping skills as far as looking after his own issues and being able to make proper decisions of how to clean up after himself? When he looks for a wife, will he need someone to babysit him or be an equal in a relationship? Some call this spoiled, but is it co-dependency coupled with anxiety? The anxiety comes from worrying about what people may think or what they might see (fear of the future).

I want to step outside of ADD to look at some of the issues we pick up with our addictive behavior. We can squeeze some control issues in here, and this seems like a good place as we are talking a little into the area of ALANON or AA. Control seems to affect us mostly for an out of control type of behavior. When we can't get people to behave in the manner that we need them to behave, we get crazy. This can be in the form of road rage, because those drivers who drive giant trucks squeeze into a spot big enough for a small car or less in front of me, I have to brake, sometimes hard, but not usually to stop from hitting them. I have to overdo it a bit with some drama by braking really hard. Now they have made me angry, and I have to chase them down, and possibly give them some hand gestures -- possibly only using one finger, or worse, following them so I can practice my stalking skills. Now somebody has taken over my body and mind by making me mad as though I am unable to control myself my own level of being mad. Pick anything that someone does or can do that will annoy you.

I was working with a client, and we had both been eating some raw carrots in the office she decided to stop, but got angry as I continued to eat quietly. I noticed that she was unable to focus, and asked why. She advised that my eating carrots was making her mad, and keeping her from focusing, I ate louder, and she got angrier. I explained, she was allowing herself to get angry because she couldn't have her own way and stop me from eating carrots. I told her to leave, and that we would continue another day. She would not leave. I needed to stop eating carrots because that's what she wanted. We also have other issues. She doesn't like sessions in my office, she wants to use the boardroom table in the outer office, and she wants to bring a swivel chair into my office instead of a regular chair. She wants to control when sessions should end, or how much work to give her to work on herself. Because she is part of a program, she has no regard for how much longer the process will take. In the past, her life partner would beat her when she would attempt to exert control over him. She comes from a family which used alcohol obsessively and had no time for her. She has been drinking and abusing drugs for twenty-five years, and she has not drank for a month and hasn't had this much sobriety since she started drinking. She tested positively for Type 6 ADD plus all the others, and has controlling tendencies and co-dependency issues. But she doesn't recognize either, believing that somebody is making her angry by doing these things to her. I'd like you to understand her sobriety is fragile right now with only a month of sobriety, the most she has had since she was thirteen. She came in only being able to string together four days of sobriety in the last year. The biggest challenge is that everything you don't like about others is merely a reflection of your own behavior.

If you are not aware of what you are doing, how can you do anything about it? I see some other issues hooked up with this. I see an egocentric attitude and apathy. Egocentric attitude is believing that everybody else sees the world the way we do. No one thinks, believes, or behaves differently in this world, do they? The apathy is having little or no regard for anyone else, just me. You could see someone fall in front of you and keep going, or if you were on Seinfeld, you might see someone steal a car from an overweight person and laugh and do nothing. I could go into a full explanation with this, but this is a book primarily about ADD and the relationship to addiction and stress-related problems. This is one that can be combated by awareness, but how do you become aware that you do this? This is where you get to go if you leave ADD untreated or choose self-medication of one form or another.

4

WHAT CAN WE DO?

"If they try to rush me, I always say, 'I've only got one other speed and it's slower.'" ~ Glenn Ford

One of the challenges that I see regularly with people and even myself is that we can get to feeling a little better, whether on our own, because anxiety and depression will ease up if we get busy doing something, especially if it is something we like to do. Sometimes the problem tends to be a famous saying we say to ourselves, "It's not that bad." From that point, we like to believe that maybe we are better, but it's certainly a lot better than it was, so I can just relax a little, I don't have to be so concerned. It's only when it's starts to get bad again that a solution is needed. I see this in our practice, at AA and in workbooks, etc. It's fine to talk about doing the work, to plan to do the work and to want to do the work, but when it comes down to doing the work, we hesitate because we know that it's hard to change and it's painful to go through some of this stuff. Why not avoid it; we are sometimes the kings and queens of procrastinating. The other hold back is that we have been struggling most of our lives by ourselves, and we are just used to suffering by ourselves, so why change now?

Another relapse problem seen is when we carry these problems for many years as much as fifty in one of my examples, the person wonders how they can carry this problem all these years and it can be changed to a painless memory in a day or two. How is that possible, it can't be true and they convince themselves, I am still suffering and what you believe can become your reality? Another common problem is not practicing the techniques we teach in coping, managing, and dealing with stressors. I am unsure if it is laziness, or unsure if it will really work, but when they leave our sessions, we have practiced and tested our work and are certain that it works. But invariably, when someone comes back as a result of struggling, there is an admission of not practicing the techniques taught. We teach a full body and brain relax triggered by two breaths to cope with stressful situations, whether remembered situations or encountered when they can't do it, we know the cause. I can't engage it, is the response, followed by I haven't been practicing.

We can also look at some issues, and notice behaviors to determine how this may fit with our overall objective. We frequently see issues such as control, anger, drama, etc. (all forms of controlling behavior) which don't have a predefined ADD application, but may be apparent in behavior, like so many behaviors which arise out of a manifestation of forms of abuse or control exerted over a client at an early age. These are usually developed as controls. In order to not allow a similar type of abuse to happen ever again, the client develops controls or behavior of their life during the abuse as a form of protection or caution to exhibit in case of a recurring type of abuse. What do I do as an adult? I flee, get really angry, have a tantrum, try to fight back, or become passive, etc. If it doesn't go well, I can resort to drama and lose it. So if I control my behavior in any manner, I may be safe. What did I do when I was a kid when you can't do any of these things, but I believe we cling to hope that maybe we could do something or we do dream of being the champion or being rescued, maybe we become a rescuer. With ADD, there may be an initial problem to begin with, or there may be a learned behavior being acted upon. I didn't go into great detail in this area, but it is also an area we work in. Our role is to teach a more appropriate response to any thinking, feeling, or behavior, or even physiological type of response.

This idea, coupled with the idea to help the person learn to practice awareness, could actually become a value (big stretch here, I can get even better by practicing awareness). Awareness sounds simple, but if we begin to pay attention to our behavior around others, especially those close to us, we could learn how annoying we can be at times. Annoying isn't too bad, but how about when we practice road rage or offering our opinions on just about anything under the sun. Sometimes, if we know a little about something, we may try to bullshit our way through as though we know a lot. See the news, and take whatever someone from another world has said or done to personally offend you. How do we learn to be aware? I don't usually know what I have done until after I have done it. It starts by starting and committing yourself preferably to a written goal and start attempting to change, and when you notice you missed the chance, committing to yourself, I will do it next time, next time. Don't try, because I think it was that famous philosopher, Yoda who said, "Try not. Do... or do not. There is no try." If you know that you are being a jerk, you are the one who is responsible for changing it. You are also responsible for being honest, and that begins with you admitting that you made a mistake and that you will do better the next time. If you keep committing to yourself, you will do better, you will. If you pretend that it didn't happen or ignore it, nothing will change. I'm sure most are familiar with people who pretend that something didn't happen or that if no one notices, it doesn't count.

This is important because, the more you unwind your life to root out these problems, the more you find to unwind. We are likened to an onion, as you peel away a layer, there is another layer underneath. The good news is that you can get to the core. Try to keep in mind that if you have had problems for twenty years, they don't go away in a couple of sessions, but it won't take twenty years.

This is looking at the world in the same manner as someone who drinks or takes drugs to escape their past hurts. The chemical abuse is a solution to help them escape from the vivid re-creation of the past. It has only become a behavior in response to a thinking and or feeling problem. Again, there may be an underlying problem of ADD, but there doesn't have to be. It just might be abuse.

There once was a TV show called, Seinfeld. In this show was a guy called, George. George was the continual recipient of whatever could go wrong, did. He was his own worst enemy in the manner he conducted his life. He cared about no one but himself. One day, he started doing the opposite of what he thought (too much thinking) he should do and started to develop using his sense or intuition, and his life changed immediately. Just a show, but I find that many of us can take a lesson from this story and stop thinking ourselves to death, and do the opposite to what we think we should do and wait and see what sort of an answer we might have if we weighed the possibilities of what we might do instead of our first thought. This is one of those things I spoke of earlier. It sounds simple, but it won't be easy. It's a choice. It's like jumping out of an airplane with a parachute. You have a choice whether you want to use the ripcord or not. It has been said that if you have one choice, you are concrete in your thinking, if you have two choices, you have a dilemma, if you have three choices, you have flexible thinking. It's like road rage. If you only know how to rage and chase someone and offer finger gestures or worse as to how they might improve their driving, you might want to learn to increase your flexibility. What are three positive options you might do instead?

One of our challenges is that we seem to see the negative side to many things. We get up in the morning, and we can start thinking about all we have to accomplish today. We start running through various scenarios, what we will do about this if that happens, etc. We may already be trying to solve problems that haven't yet occurred. When we have concerns about what is going to happen in the future, we may be looking at anxiety. Why can't we get up and believe that we could have a good day?

At times, we may appear as oppositional or rebelling against someone's ideas or attempts to force us do something their way, and we just dig our heels in. It can also provide that little bit of chaos to help us through that difficult moment.

If we wake up in the morning and start thinking, I don't feel that great or I don't want to go to work, a whole bunch of reasons start appearing as why you shouldn't go to work. The best is feeling sick. This is an excuse to stay in bed. A lot of times when a person wants to remain in bed and sleep or just curl up, it is depression.

On a recent morning, my wife getting up awakened me. I am usually up first, as I like to exercise, usually jogging. So off she goes to shower, etc. I lay in bed trying to go back to sleep, which is past my time normally. I lay there for an hour trying to sleep, which I never do. I sensed that something wasn't right, but went through a series of what's troubling me. Oh, also, I was a bit whiney. I had a couple of things on my mind which were a bit troublesome. I had to go somewhere that day where I don't like a key person who was going to be there. I didn't want to go. I also had a client who needed to restore her position in her family, otherwise they wanted no part of her. She drinks and denies it and tries to hide it with strong mouthwash. I saw her the other day, and she smelled of alcohol and strong mouthwash, but I had told her, she would stop when she was ready. We were past the time of stopping the drinking. I suggested she needed to tell me when she needs to drink and I would coach her through this stage. Our last session, she smelled of liquor at nine a.m. and denied drinking for the last week. I prefer the truth, and then I can help. This was the same thing that her family accuses her of doing. I was tempted to tell her I couldn't help her unless she wants to stop, not her family wanting her to stop and not me wanting her to stop.

I tried to take a couple of deep breaths, which is my technique for gaining a full body relax complete with a place I go to relax, a picture triggered by the breaths. No, not working, tried several times. I finally engaged it and figured I had some low-grade depression going on. I finally got up and wondered why and tried to go through my life and figure what was going on, what was I angry about? So I took a couple of more deep breaths and got dressed and went. It was downright cold out there (0 degrees or 32 Fahrenheit). Now I also realized I had some anxiety going on as well. I kept taking two breaths, and I was now good to go. I started jogging and said my prayer and cleared my mind of everything, and when I got back I was still a bit off but much better. I was showering and my wife got home and brought me two coffees, an ice coffee from MacDonald's, and a hot (decaf which is better for my head) coffee as well. Well I was happy now. We headed off to church; I grabbed a banana and peanut butter as it really helps when I'm off. By now, I realized it was more than a little bit of depression, maybe a lot. I had no idea where it comes from; I hadn't seen anything like this for a long time, maybe a year or two and anxiety on top of it. Once I was sort of calmed down I could reason with myself a bit better, and consider the high action movie (John Wick) I saw last night or the candy I had been stuffing in myself as Halloween was two days before. I don't do well with a lot of sugar, but I eat it anyway at times, sometimes too much. Anyhow, I also decided as I am writing this book, I have been asking GOD to help me and I decided maybe this is what he wanted me to be able to explain, and it is easier if I know what I am talking about. This was about five hours later and I was fine now but I knew that in the old days, I would have gone into hiding and probably tried to be angry with anyone who would dare to try and offer help or attempt to reason with me or even have the nerve to slow me down in traffic. Life is good too today if I let it be. It was great, a baptism of friends of ours, visit some old friends, some lunch. This was my first challenge of this size in a couple of years, still some remnants of spectrum bi-polar. My stuff only works 99.95% of the time if you work it.

One of my friends calls my strategies quick fixes. I can change my mind and my mood and get on with life, or be a miserable person who nobody wants to be around, or maybe I'll just avoid people for a while. The last time my friend had a bout of depression, it lasted months. This method may not be perfect because we are the weakness in it, and it may not work every time, but it is almost foolproof if you learn it, practice it, and work it. Sometimes, even I forget and stumble (today) but I never lost it, not even on myself. We are not trying to be perfect; we are striving to be a better person. A glitch once in a while is far better than once in a while having a good day, but having a glitch most of the time.

My good friend says that these are the cards we are dealt. We don't get any others, and it is unfortunate that we may have suffered some setbacks and in some cases really serious ones, but these are the only cards we get. We need to learn how to play them as there are no others going to be dealt to us. I get it, some days we just like to whine a little, and feeling sorry for ourselves is just a sign of depression, but some days when this is the feeling, you have got to shake it off. No one else can. No matter how much someone feels bad for you, it is always going to come down to, what are you going to do?

Some might tell you that ADD comes from genetic damage from somewhere up the family tree where someone had ADD or abused substances and damaged their brain and mine as well. This is the way it is, crying and gnashing of teeth doesn't change it. You can try to improve your life, and while you have children, or will in the future, you can be prepared to go that extra step for them and change yourself to cope, manage, and deal with it.

5

SOME IDEAS

"The best non-pharmacological treatment for ADD is exercise, sex, and humor."~ Dr. Ned Hallowell, Co-author of Driven to Distraction.

I can offer some suggestions, everything under options will be challenging to accomplish, but it will help you to find peace and maybe happiness. Look at what you have been doing; has it been working for you so far? Change only comes with work.

A GOOD START

Diet

- Avoid starchy food (potatoes, bread, pasta, sugar, or stimulants to excess).
- Eat protein every meal and a protein snack about 3: 30 or 4 p.m.
- Eat vegetables every meal.
- Eat fresh fruit for snacks.

Supplements

- Many good supplements can be found to treat depression and anxiety.
- Cooking with Saffron helps lower depression.
- Try 5-hydroxytryptophan and gamma-amino butyric acid, more commonly known as 5-HTP and GABA.
- Tyrosine for Types one and two.

Exercise

- Develop an exercise program to help get blood flowing through your body, especially to your brain to help rebuild it.
- Question your negative thoughts, is that true, does this problem apply to me, etc.
- Develop a goal list of what you want to accomplish (review daily)
- Individual plans for each goal (school or profession, mental well being, family relations, financial affairs, fitness, career, friendships, spiritual, etc.). What are you going to do? Do a life plan to help determine your skills.
- Time line for start and completion. Don't get too stuck on completion for as soon as you involve other people, it changes.
- Picture yourself in the future accomplishing what you want.

Options: add any of these to your list

- Our Workshop
- One on One Sessions
- Dynamic Discovery, a process of self-evaluation (Cheap)
- Dynamic Discovery, a process of self-evaluation, Workbook (Cheap)

Or develop a strategy for being able to relax or change your mind (mood) and get on with your goals for the day, which should be part of your overall goals to become a better person which should include some of your new values.

Considering supplements or medications and dosage is something that may be revealed as a result of testing and consultation with a doctor whether medical, holistic, or naturopath, but not based on ideas gained from books, the Internet, or a friend's advice. Before mixing supplements with prescription medications, a medical doctor should be consulted.

ADD OVERVIEW OF SUPPLEMENTS (DOSAGE AND USAGE DETERMINED BY YOUR HEALTH CARE PROFESSIONAL).

ADD Type 1 and 2 are viewed as a shortage of Dopamine within your system.

- Some solutions can be Rhodiola, Ginseng, Ashwagadha, green tea, grapeseeed extract, Acetyl-L-Cartine, or L-Tyrosine. Again solutions or dosages vary according to individuals.

ADD Type 3 (Over-focused) are viewed as a Dopamine and Serotonin shortage

- Some solutions can be St. Johns Wort, which works on many to decrease hyperactivity, but can conflict with other types of ADD, especially Type 6 and Type 5, and cause serious issues (side effects) as well as with Type 4, which requires other supplements. Trytophan which is found in milk and eggs and 5-HTP.

ADD Type 4 Temporal lobe can be viewed as learning and behavioral problems, aggression, or decreased activity in lobes (common head injury problems).

- Some solutions are Gingko, Vinpocetine, Phosphatylserine, GABA, Magnesium Citrate or Magnesium Taurate, Huperzine A, Acetyl-L-Carnitine, N-Acetylsteine, or Alpha Lipoic Acid.

ADD Type 5 Considered as overactive (ADD and Depression linked together), can be negative.

- Some solutions can be DL-Phenylanine, L-Tyrosine, or SAMe. Do use for Bi-Polar or Type 6

ADD Type 6 Many parts of the brain are hyperactive or disinhibited. Alcohol use is dangerous. Can be Bi-Polar and ADD together or other types of ADD. Opposite of others which are usually decreased activity. Can be cyclical.

- No St Johns Wort.
- Some solutions might be GABA, 5-HTP, L-Tyrosine, or Fish Oil.

ADD Type 7 Anxious, too much brain activity, avoidance of conflict, and insecurity.

- Some solutions might be Vitamin B6, Inistol,
- L-Thaenine, Relora, Magnesium, or Holy Basil.

6

HOW ABOUT A PLAN

"Say What You Mean and Mean What You Say." ~ Barbara Coloroso

A lot of this will work on kids with ADD, and also with ADD adults – as long as you're interested in doing the work. Think of the following statement as a method of encouraging those close to you and a message for yourself.

BEST INTEREST

IF SELF = BEST INTEREST,

Then who is the best person to look after your best interest?

For these purposes, best interest is defined as not being deliberately hurtful or harmful to self or others; others may choose to feel hurt, but that is their choice.

What can we do...

If you have read this book, you are obviously looking for answers. The book can be the beginning of finding a way through the maze of what is out there. Unfortunately, there are no quick fixes, but diet, supplements and exercise are a beginning to help stabilize behaviour and thinking. Trying to change anything before this stage is a waste of time. A lot of times, we are dealing with someone who is also capable of being impulsive and maybe oppositional, as well as some other traits. Impulsive people are not really prone to sitting still, either inside their head or behaviour wise. You might say, this book is not about ADD but it is a start in the right direction – as long as there is consistency from you and good discipline that can help you change things for yourself and others.

We use experiential learning throughout our programs; coaching, workshops and workbooks. Our brain doesn't realize whether we actually do something physically or just do it mentally. All the brain knows is whether we were able to do it. This is how we remember how to do something because it is through repetition and not by simply memorizing. Anyone who has been in the military will understand this concept as that is how it is done. You do something repetitively until it is ingrained in your head and it is a reflex. We then do it. This is the reason I suggest you do something with different examples of real life memories. We can practise in our heads how to redo problems or set goals and at some point we will know how to do it. Because there are a number of steps involved, it will be a challenge, there is a challenge to getting better or behaving differently. There is also a goal setting exercise a little further into this chapter which you can use to put this into play.

I would suggest the same for our workbook. The workbook can help you change your behaviour and thinking, but if you were never much for sitting down and focussing on doing detailed work, what makes you think things have changed? Especially if you decide to have a piece of white bread with jam on it for a snack, because your focus will be gone (carbs and sugar). The workbook can be used on your kids but they might not have the baggage and need for much of the work. But the goal setting and problem solving works well, and future goals and the Darn Good Start exercise is useable.

I believe there is a need for education in this field, especially if you have children or plan to. You will need some help or you will raise them exactly like you were and, if you were an ADD child, they will likely be ADD, too. This book is the beginning not the "be all".

Feeling bad about what you had to suffer through can stop whenever you decide you want a good future. Or you can wait until the future arrives and you are totally unprepared for it and it didn't work out in the manner you expected.

I would suggest taking a look at a simple goal setting exercise at this point and decide what can be done while reading this book to achieve the direction you want to follow. This is also a good exercise to teach your kids, and maybe a spouse if there is struggle in their life or even yourself if anyone has some focus issues. Well maybe it isn't simple the first time but it can be a life changer. Necessary for an ADD life.

- State your goal in positive terms, such as, "What do I want?"
- Self evaluate your goal. Are you doing this for yourself or someone else?
- Define your goal; Where, when and how will this happen and with whom do I want this?
- Describe the details of the process: What will I be doing to get my goal? How will I know I am achieving it? What will I see, hear and feel when I have it?
- Identify the resources you need: What resources do I have now? What resources do I need to acquire? Have I ever achieved this goal or something like it before? What happens if I act as though I already have it?
- Is your goal ecological? What is the real purpose behind why you want this goal? What will you lose or gain if you have it? What will and won't happen if you get it? What will and won't happen if you don't get it?
- Describe the first step you will take towards achieving you goal?

Perhaps, you wanted to change your life to be able to cope with ADD or depression, be a better parent or spouse; if so, what would you look like in about six months if you were able to change? What would you do, if you knew you could not fail? Think about what would happen if you actually succeed. Do this first and consider how you will use the book to actually plan or follow the exercise while reading book.

Feeling bad about what you actually had to suffer through as a child and part of your adult life can stop whenever you decide you want to have a good future – or you can wait and see what ever fate or circumstance drops in your lap and continue in your current fashion, which may include that inability to cope, manage or deal with problems. We can use the past to learn from and then put it behind us, but we cannot change it.

Many of us have learned through a bribe, reward, or punishment system. It could be praise, material stuff or offering love or removing it. This may have caused us to learn false values as this becomes an expectation when we decide to either do something or not do it. They could withhold or we could withhold, depending on who wanted the upper-hand the most.

We want much for our children even the worst of parents. It's how we go about teaching our kids through our unconscious role-modelling that is how they learn. For example, beat your spouse in front of your kids and watch what they do when they get married and life gets challenging. By the way, this takes a little time into the future for you to see the results but I would ask you to take my word on this at least for now. If we make all their decisions for them, we merely teach our kids to be co-dependent. This can become a problem for them in later life if all they are used to is being told what to do, and they will then attempt to do what they learned (control others.) If that isn't enough of a down side, consider that they will be unable to make good decisions on their own as they have no experience and don't know how. This provides them the opportunity to make poor life-decisions when nobody is around to tell them what to do. Many people seek to find control in their lives by drinking or drugging as a means to having control in their lives and perhaps as a coping technique for when they make bad decisions or they hurt inside. Kids also learn from watching their parents drink or drug.

Learning to not save them all the time from everything that befalls them may be painful for you but it will help them stand on their own. Part of life is about being able to ask for help when you need it, not waiting to be rescued, which only encourages helplessness. If we wait on them and enable them to behave in any inappropriate way, they will be lost when on their own, or they will need to hook up with a rescuer-type person (another form of co-dependence) – usually a drunk or enabler. An example might be: "I can't eat this", and you find something they prefer. Or, "I don't have to accept my part here, I can negotiate or withhold my happiness." Or maybe clothes aren't picked up and put in the hamper. If you yell and say, "You didn't pick up your clothes", and then pick them up for them. They are learning that they don't have to live up to their responsibilities. And they don't really have to listen to you and your credibility for keeping your word is gone. If they run out of clean clothes and go to school smelly a couple of times and get sent home or teased, they might learn. Might. Another lesson could be that they might have to do their own laundry when it is that bad and you could teach them how. The rule can be, if it is not in the hamper, clothes do not get washed. A parent's job is not to enable their children to live their life in any way they want but with responsibility to prepare them for adult life on their own.

We help them make better decisions by encouraging, influencing, providing feedback and the development of good habits (discipline). You might want to look up this word and see what it really means. This helps them to learn things can be okay and what you can do to solve or resolve your problems instead of, now what do we or I do about this, and maybe drink. If you teach them how to communicate and let them practise with you, they will learn negotiation and how to influence decisions. If you beat them, they will beat others. Many of us have learned there is a bribe or reward or maybe a punishment system. It took less of these kinds of lessons to learn how to do this or how to avoid punishment, for we learn quickly when we feel threatened but the good quality lessons we learn by practising are more difficult – especially on the teacher or leader. When teaching one's children, we need to allow for mistakes, for if mistakes are not tolerated, we can only learn how to operate under perfectionist standards. Mistakes are how we learn best as that gives us the experience of knowing what can go wrong and how to avoid life mistakes.

Kids are going to make mistakes, and maybe some big ones at times. This will always be about your kids and they will always be in a learning mode. Whatever you do to them or for them will be how they raise your grandchildren. If they make a big mistake and you punish them for it, they will remember. That form of openness with communication with you may not be repeated. They may tell you because they were looking for support and help in solving a major problem. Our love for them needs to be unconditional from day one, not just when they are good. I am not saying you need to solve the problem or get them out of it. After all, it is still their problem, and maybe you can help them go through the steps of problem solving.

Drugs and alcohol may be one of the problems which appear. You may know nothing about the topic but as a common sense person, you might seek the help of an expert in the field in case you are asked for it. But think of this; how much advice do you ever follow when someone tries to solve your problem(s)? That is my point; we rarely take solicited advice let alone unsolicited advice. Unfortunately, we sometimes see advice givers as a "know-it-all", and that is not a good place to be. Providing support is being there and being willing to help when asking what you can do to help. Alcohol and drug abuse can be seen as a sign of a problem for which drugs or alcohol is their solution because their coping skills are limited.

We are attempting to teach our kids how to make choices, preferably smart ones. This learning can occur early in life when it comes to getting dressed. Initially we can offer two simple choices so the choice is easier when limited. When offering other choices, it can also be somewhat limited, such as a form of corrective discipline. If you are going to do that, then you will be going to your room or the corner. "If/then" choices can be very powerful when encouraging proper behaviour. At an early age, whether they match their clothing or not will not physically harm them. It may offend your sense of propriety but no one will be hurt in the making of this memory. If you recall, raising kids is not about you but about them, and doing it well.

We can start out small with decision making at an early age and, to help them advance, we can increase their choices and responsibilities along the way. This will be of service to you when it comes to their making good choices, such as friendships and when chemical choices come into their lives.

It has been said that we use chemicals in later life as a means to help us cope with the lack of good parenting when we were small. If they learned hostility, violence and anger from you, let's hope they don't practise on you when they are bigger and stronger and tougher from being knocked around. If we want them to learn joy, happiness and understanding, we must teach it and practice it.

Mistakes are feedback as well as encouragement for when you get knocked down and you know enough to get back up again. We will get back up anyway but many will get back up cursing and swearing and grumbling for awhile afterwards. Is it better to get up and get on with life or do we need to dwell on poor me or look for sympathy from others (is this drama)? When we think of establishing patterns of appropriate behaviour, we can think of forms of encouragement for correct behaviour and correcting incorrect behaviour. But we have to be able to, "Say What We Mean and Mean What We Say," to quote that famous author Barbara Coloroso, who knows more about raising healthy kids than anyone in the world according to me. We cannot make empty threats such as, "You will do this or you'll be grounded for a year." First, that might be a bit excessive, and not much better if you change your mind and weaken your stance for a couple of reasons. What parent wants their kids at home continuously for a year? Secondly, if you don't live up to what you say, you have lost credibility and they have learned that keeping your word isn't that important. There goes integrity.

The following questions represent a problem solving method that we teach to adults and young people, but may be a little involved for really young people. This is a problem solving method that you can use anywhere and anytime as it provides a lot of insight into good problem solving. Implement it in stages for adults and teenagers, and slowly introduce it to the younger folks over a longer period of time. As with all good things, the sooner the better.

WHAT DO I WANT?

- What is that going to do for me?
- What's stopping me?
- What is important to me here?
- What's working well?
- What can be better?
- What resources are going to support me?

There is nothing easy about this solution but neither are life's problems. I suggest you use this on yourself until you've really got it and then use it on someone else – but be able to explain it.

If you are struggling with teaching a lesson or concept and the feedback is positive but there is a confused look on their face, you might be going about it in the wrong way. That is the beauty of getting them to practice what they have learned; if they can't do it, you failed, they didn't. Perhaps freshening your approach to the problem is what is needed. If you keep teaching in a negative fashion, maybe all you are teaching is negative behaviour and thinking.

If you want them to grow up with confidence and self-esteem, they will need to know how to accomplish tasks by setting goals and making plans on how to succeed at the goals. Your ability to provide leadership and encouragement through much of these skills will be beneficial for you as you can hone your skills at the same time. This provides an opportunity for them to learn right from wrong by seeing it in action and, if you nurture an openness in them, they might learn and retain more than at an ethics class, or in church once a week. If you remember much about school, memorization was great for tests but how much were you able to practice of what you learned under pressure?

If we want them to learn appropriate behaviour it will be through continual repetition of a positive behaviour of any sort. Sometimes we criticize but it may appear as harsh to our kids because our intentions do not always impact someone younger and more sensitive than we might be today as opposed how we were when we were younger. Words to remember might be, impact not intent. During my days in the reserve forces, I worked with cadets (children) and I learned sarcasm is not a good teacher. Kids may not understand whether we are being funny or mean. This can leave them in a confused state and they may take away the wrong message and practice it in the wrong way. It won't do much to enhance the learning experience.

Many employers practice corrective discipline. We want to separate behaviour from the person. They may have done something wrong but it may have been a mistake; it was what they did that is the problem not them. If we teach them about good habits and how to correct mistakes when they occur, we can expect good discipline to be is learned most of the time. I was involved in a company I started and developed a simple three step method of correcting mistakes, which is easier than criticizing someone or making them feel they are inferior.

1. Review what happened from your perspective and seek agreement. I like to get this in writing as whatever someone writes usually sticks in their head.
2. Review what was expected. Ask what happened from their perspective.
3. What could be done differently in the future to gain correct result? Encourage or lead with the answer to the question if need be, but it needs to be their own words. This can become a commitment.

There are no losers in this type of a situation. This provided a supportive environment with encouragement, an opportunity for communication, the acceptance of mistakes with an opportunity to learn and think for yourself. Even kids know that there has to be consequences for mistakes or wrongful conduct since this is what happens in the real world. Don't tell them that they screwed up and then coddle them when they are crying. When they are older, that's not what happens at school or at work. We ought not do this when they are small, either; if they need to go to the corner or their room for a time out, coddling afterwards undoes whatever we did.

I remember when I was a kid and wanted to do something my parents might not approve of. At times their opinions ruled my life and, when I got to my teen years, I disregarded going to them first and got the haircut I wanted or whatever I decided I wanted to do. I did many things out of defiance because I knew what they would and would not approve. In retrospect, I didn't go bizarre because I still had to live with my actions. I would have been more on side with them with their realization that no one would be hurt by my actions, just maybe their opinions. Some approval can be good for kids – or at least acceptance, because it is too late anyway to undo.

There are two things occurring here and one is about oppositional behaviour and the other is about where communication skills were lacking. I see somewhat of a relationship between the two. I resisted being told what to do, which I speak to in a few short paragraphs. The communication needs to have two parties being involved in any discussion. Most of the communication with my parents was from them without feedback from me. I was not allowed to speak my mind or disagree out of fear of reprisal, which could have been physical violence at worst, but my disagreement was not left unchecked. My mother beat my older brother and me when he was eighteen and I was fourteen with an electric cord for lying about eating a cinnamon bun. I ate it but by this age I wasn't giving that up, never; I wouldn't give her the satisfaction.

Communication needs to be a family experience so that both sides can share equally with movement up or down, there has to be equality, at least for the discussion. There can be disagreement, but in the end, negotiation can change, unfairness can be a change ingredient, but it must be voiced. However, it can only be voiced in an area where open communication is tolerated. Small people live in the land of the giants and are already at a disadvantage without the adult raising their voice. A family meeting should be an opportunity for openness and honesty. When this is about openness, an expression of feelings can be shared. This is a time to disregard one's opinions or judgements about whatever and allow open mindedness, allow yourself to be convinced or not. Openness can lead to good sharing but is not a place for allowing someone to feed you a load of bullshit, not that anyone ever tried that. The meeting should not be rushed by either party having commitments some place else. This can help your kids in being articulate about what their concerns are, as far as negotiating, and a communication builder.

I opened the door to oppositional behaviour and spoke to it briefly as negative talk. We use it to create chaos which feeds us a quantity of adrenalin. Whether we come equipped with this as standard equipment or it is learned behaviour as a way of us dealing with too much calmness in our heads and we need some excitement doesn't matter. This is the idea that we can immediately come up with an argument to just about anything someone can say. I use to like to get into political debates, abortion, or religious discussion and I would sometimes ask, which side do you want. I would just use the opposite of what they would say. We have the ability to see the negative side about anything. We can turn on someone close to us if our mood is off for this will get us out of depression to a degree. That is what adrenalin does but that is merely anxiety. We get addicted to this use of our internally controlled drug at an early age.

This "addiction" can be partially overcome by developing a list of three things a day (non material things) we are grateful about for twenty-one days. Write these down so you do not repeat. Then do five things to be grateful about for thirty days; again write it down. This will give you a new perspective to help you change your negative thoughts into positive thoughts.

I work as a life-coach for people with ADD, Addictions, PTSD and other forms of stress management. I find that the people suffering these sorts of problems at times have inflexibility. I usually help develop flexibility by reviewing past choices in situations. I get clients to generate three new learning experiences that they may use in the future to make better choices. That can also turn a negative situation into a positive one because learning from a bad experience turns it into positive ending. I also use this with bad dreams by saying, "Tell me three things you can learn from this dream that might help you in the future." I sometimes have to qualify this by saying, "Perhaps there is a concept involved in the dream of a problem in your life and your sub-conscious is showing you how to find the answer." It works.

If someone tells you what to do, how do you feel about that? For me it can be annoying or irritating. Think about what you feel when it occurs with you. I'm unsure whether to call this nagging or controlling. Think of a time it happened to you; how did you feel? Same with kids or spouses. If someone asks you to do something, you might be more apt to do it willingly than the resentment you might feel when being ordered or told. Same for spouses and kids.

Some of this stuff I speak of may be annoying to many of you. Which puts me in the area of opinions. Opinions are dangerous because we either agree or become upset. It's like the news reporters on television. When they start offering opinions, it is an attempt to get us involved in their station, to sell commercials through ratings. If it happens enough, we will begin to watch with a new enthusiasm. This form of reporting is designed to get you involved and annoy or anger you. This is our adrenalin friend, the fight or flight drug, which we like to use. But we are not going off to war, we are going to drive and we are already irritated, and we haven't left yet. We can have road rage. Do we do this with each other when we have conflicting ideas or opinions? When someone disagrees with us, do we become annoyed or upset? Children for the most part are adaptive at earlier years but, as they age, they seem to lose their adaptability, and more so as they approach senior citizen status. Hopefully they don't learn this from us and it's just a factor of aging. They learn to stay on your good side and if they contain their ability to gather information and be open to changing their minds with fresh knowledge, they can become less close minded or opinionated like us. In other words if they develop similar ideas about politics, sports, news, etc. will they just become a clone of you?

Unfortunately, opinions are usually negative thoughts which can encourage arguments which again lead back to the fight or flight drug. The other unfortunate thought about adrenalin is, it also can lead to over use and generate anxiety. Does this encourage thinking or does it mean, "Think what I want you to think"?

Where do we teach responsibility? We can give them chores to perform that can be taught with the simple use of goal setting. It seems involved with something so simple as taking out the garbage or helping clean up the dishes when we are young. The earlier the training, the more acceptance learned. In order to live in a community, we have to pay taxes and contribute as good citizens and help each other out at times. We have to learn to be friendly, cut our grass and shovel snow. Does anyone pay you to do this? But we are willing to pay our kids for doing the same thing. What do they pay us for the food we provide? Or the place to sleep or the place to entertain? We give them an allowance for eating and sleeping with us. We give them tasks to perform, whether dishes or cutting the grass, and they grow with the expectations that they must be paid for doing community work in order to be a part of this family. "No," we say, "we are teaching them how to manage money and work for what they earn." How does that teach anyone responsibility to contribute to the family? When you get sent off to the old folks home, will they even come to visit you or will you still have to pay them for helping in your community? The learning here is, you can't do something unless you get a reward. This doesn't encourage a sense of accomplishment or responsibility if they get paid. If you want to give them an allowance, give it but don't use it as a bribe or a gift with strings attached. The lessons learned today, stay for a long time. Also know that change doesn't come easily after we age a few years.

The learning of responsibility helps us to control our lives to give us that sense of control in later life. We know what we can expect from life if we contribute. Sort of like a computer, if I do this I get this, instead of I don't do anything unless I get something for it. Learning how to take responsibility will work well in marriage or relationships.

CONCLUSION

"To invent, you need a good imagination and a pile of junk." ~ Thomas Edison

I also speak to the program called, Alcoholics Anonymous (AA). I have been involved in the AA program for a number of years, and I truly believe in it. I have learned much about fellowship and friendship. The foundations of the Big Book and companion book called, The Twelve by Twelve are excellent resources to find sobriety, as some of us pick up some addictive issues in our journey with ADD, PTSD, etc. The difficulties I find are more with the various interpretations and practices different people plug into the literature and subsequent programs. And because they have been in the program for a while, we give them credibility, but many of them still struggle to change behaviors in spite of twenty or thirty years of seniority. There are various interpretations and spoken words a new person learns about. When you find a meeting you feel comfortable with, stay there and try it for a while. If you decide against it, try another. I suggest that you try several at the beginning, and then make a decision. A person who is working the steps and working at changing their life and seriously attending meetings will not wonder why the program doesn't work. This is a program which can help you, like any other program, but a person has to work it. I hear of many suggestions of working the steps of how you must do this. Get Twelve Steps Twelve Traditions, and find out yourself. If someone is still struggling after ten or fifteen years, what would make you think they have the answer and try to be a sponsor? Research your sponsor and make sure that this person makes sense when sharing. Some people find that they can run groups or be sponsors to people and they may be very knowledgeable about the program, but when we find a solution, does it mean that it is the only solution? Or do you have continue learning and developing to try and take yourself further? This can be a simple program, but like anything else, people can make it into their own creation. My friend says, "It's a simple program but don't confuse simple with easy." The criticisms you may notice in this book are not of the AA program, but of the many forms people have turned it into. If you have to, continue to do step four where your inability to cope with something going on in your life is dependent on you continually asking for help from GOD. When I first tried to change or correct road rage, I was pulling over every couple of minutes to pray for help because so many people were pissing me off, but it was my problem not theirs. It's also pretty hard in rush hour traffic as well. I can accept that idea, but why do I have to find out what happened to me that caused me to be angry each and every time. This is anxiety. Why can't we just learn to relax, change our moods or our minds, and then sort out the problem, why am I like this? We can use all of our brain instead of part of it, because most of it is locked up in stress mode. If you are not a hard drinker or a drug abuser whether recreational or prescription, you might try Alanon.

Educating yourself by doing some research into this whole ADD idea can be beneficial. I began my quest with Daniel Amen's "Healing ADD" book and just kept going from there. His material made a lot more sense than most. He wrote to average people who could understand him, and he had easy to use basic ideas from diet to simple techniques to make changes from within. He also has a website and a weekly newsletter, which he will send to you if you request from his website. Even if that is as far as you can go, you are a lot further than you were yesterday.

George talks about this stuff we do being like the fountain of youth. I notice that I do have a spring in my step again, and I look at the world very differently. I like it a lot. I look forward to accomplishing every day. I still jog, have a light workout, and try to eat well. If I don't have a too much client stuff, sessions, texting or emailing with them, I work on doing some writing, whether a blog or a new book, training myself or reading text type books. This is what makes the difference in my life which makes yesterday so different from today. If I have objectives for the day and the future, I am not worried about the past (depression) or the future (anxiety). I keep busy even in the evening. I spend an hour reading, training, or writing. Figure it out, I have a busy brain and if I don't keep it busy, it could run amuck. I don't care if I have to work until I am dead, I enjoy it and what would an old guy do, sit in my rocking chair, go to a bar, hang around with old people and do nothing, I don't think so.

If you are looking for a workbook which can help you to learn some techniques to help you change, check out our ADD/ADHD workbook. Combine some changes with diet and exercise, and who knows what could happen for you.

Once you begin your recovery process, imagine yourself to be healthy and functioning well with maybe a goal of self-awareness. If you can be cognizant of your unwanted behaviors or even for something you just did, you can set that up as a goal (state it in positive terms) as to what your life might be like without that behavior. Don't try to do too many of these things at once, and be sure to write them down so you can keep track of changes you make from within. This will be challenging, unless you use at least a workbook or a notebook.

I believe that if we start to look at this ADD thing as an attribute instead of a negative in our life and focus on what can I do, we will learn to live and adapt. This is the way it is, and we need to learn to adapt, or our negative beliefs will ultimately destroy us or at least our minds. We ADDers think too much, and if we focus on thinking too much about what is wrong with us, it will become a bigger problem rather than acceptance of who we are. But these are just words, what are you going to do about it, and when do you start? What results will you see in three, six, and twelve months? Try to imagine what you will look like without these problems. Yes, that soon.

I spoke about awareness earlier, but I want to go back to it. We have to develop an awareness of our bodies (physiology) and our thinking, behaving, and doing. A do it yourself version which can supplement your training today might be to become aware of myself. I need to pay attention to what I am doing. An example might be when showering, pay attention to the water and its movement over you, its temperature as it touches your skin, feel the different sensations as you lather yourself and how much smoother the washcloth or the brush feels on your skin, and feel the rinse as you remove the soap. Feel the water on different parts of your body. See the light and colors around you, the soap, cloth, water, etc. Just focus on the shower, not what you are going to do later or what you did before. Focus on the job you are trying to complete right now, and how that fits into your scheme of things of how much better you will be in three months. Try to see, think, feel, and behave for every job you have to do, and notice the impact it has on you, and how you feel afterwards knowing that you were able to clear your mind.

This can be the same as a simple form of meditating. Practice laying in bed or sitting in a chair and try to notice all the sounds you might hear, the different forms of eye stimulation around you, the feel of the chair or bed on different parts of your body, covers or clothing, what can you smell or taste, and what your hands are touching. Allow yourself to just enjoy the world around you, and remember to force any thinking out of your head. Give yourself some time to just slow down and breathe in to the count of four and out to the count of four. Hold your girlfriend's or your spouse's hand, and actually feel it, feel the warmth of it, the softness, the texture of the skin, look at her or him, see the very reasons you signed on, and wonder what they are all about, listen to her or him when they speak, the tone, the sounds, and you might learn about yourself when you do this.

When I first became a policeman, I learned that I had to make notes and keep track of whatever happened as it might come back to a court case down the road. The oldest case I was ever called back for was about eleven years after I left the police, and the incident was about four years before that. I am talking about something that may never happen to most of us. But we learn in school, and believe me that was a really long time ago. We learned to take notes so that we could remember stuff that we might run across again such as tests or exams. In business, we need to keep notes about discussions with clients or discipline sessions with employees as it must be entered on their file as soon as we get an opportunity, especially if their file is in the office and we don't get there until later. I also use a notebook to keep track of the lists I create with things I need to do or when I get an idea that I need to follow up later. I just can't seem to remember everything I need to do or remember without some form of help.

Today, they give kids agendas in school. I need one or a phone that will do it all. It is also like important dates such as family birthdays or my anniversary or dates I make to see clients or friends. I need to put them in my phone. In times gone by, I used a planner with a calendar in it to write important dates or I would forget and miss it and then feel bad when it happened. This is something where people feel disappointed in us when we forget their importance with us. It saves on wear and tear on us because when we get busy, we focus on what we are doing such as prioritizing instead of what it was I was to remember. My ex-wife got annoyed with me as I would bring home the same gift like flowers for a few years for our anniversary or a birthday as I would remember at the last minute and it was all I could do was to get my friend to sell me flowers at the end of the day.

When I would make a list of the things I had to do in a day, I would decide which things had to be completed for sure that day. The remaining items would go to the top of the next day's list. This was important as if I simply followed the list as it was written, which I was certainly capable of, I might miss something important. As the size of my business grew to include three other cities with one hundred and sixty employees, I had a lot to remember, and didn't always to a good job at that. I need to recognize or be aware that I had problems. Your wife may (eventually) forgive you, but clients and teachers are not so easy going.

I sometimes like to put things off until the last moment, such as getting gas. I sometimes would see the gas gauge and realize I needed gas, but would sometimes put it off as I was in a hurry or it was just the end of the day and I just want to get home. The next day, I was a little slow getting going in the morning and got out to my vehicle and would see the gas was low and consider should I try and make my appointment and get gas later? I had run out of gas a couple of times in this scenario, and I was really late and of course felt a bit stupid because it was preventable. If I were to blow off an important appointment, I could beat myself up for awhile and I don't mean minutes or hours. I could blow this way out of proportion or I could know better and have gassed up before now. If you sit and wait for a tow or walk to get gas, you can horribly abuse your ego in this time space. If you say to yourself, I am such a loser enough times, you will start believing it and it will stick. Nowadays, I remember that lesson, but whenever I make a mistake in this new life, I exam the incident and try to find three lessons I can learn from the experience. I then have a better chance of remembering and correcting the incident for the future.

I also have to make lists when I go shopping, as I will forget what I started out to buy and get home and realize what I was meant to get. I can almost see the dumb look on my face when I walk in the door without what I went to get, and then have to explain to my wife why I was going back to the store again. It's almost like when I go shopping, I see so much excitement in looking at all the stuff, especially in the produce section. It's all so colorful and smells good and feels good. So many of my senses are involved, it's such an experience. Sometimes I can go out for milk or something else simple, I could be gone for a long time and bring home extra stuff. I realize that this probably sounds silly but when I start looking around, I check out desserts and maybe sandwich meats and who knows what else, freshly cooked soup which I have to smell. Some parts of me still act like a kid, so I make a list and before I leave, I also find out how pressing the need is so I know when to be back. However, if I go shopping as I am making dinner, I get what I need and I am gone as I have another task (cooking).

All these ideas might require some switching around for varied parts of my life whether work or play, shopping, or just trying to be responsible. We all have to find our way, but these things can be changed up to suit individual needs. I need my life to be simple at times, as I can sure make it complicated, especially when I get behind or forget something, and then the pressure or stress is there and I can easily forget.

I found a way to get some peace in my head from anxiety. I have been working on not having opinions about what people say to me, or listening to the news and getting into a heated exchange in my head with no one. These are judgments, for we may think we know better and judgments are a way of trying to protect ourselves or create a better life for someone else or whatever, they are judgments which occupy our brain for what? This gives you anxiety or works you up for what. How do stop it. Practice shutting your mind off that, change the channel, shut your mouth, and just breathe and count to ten.

You can be or do anything you want as long as it doesn't hurt anyone including you. It's like having an idea of what you want, then a choice of how you will do it, and then doing it.

My bibliography can also be viewed as a reading list because these are some of the books which have helped me on my journey. Writing this has been enjoyable for me.

I hope that you have found this book informative. I would love if you could head back to Amazon and leave a review.

Please check out our website there is great information on it and also several free book downloads on various subjects. If you need any further help please contact me at

www.bobbrayauthor.com or www.dynamicdiscovery.ca

ATTENTION DEFICIT DISORDER IN ADULTS WORKBOOK

BOB BRAY & GEORGE BISSETT

INTRODUCTION

This is a book about change. That is one of the topics that many of us are uncomfortable doing or even thinking. We don't like it because of the uncertainty of where it will take us and it will be hard. We like our life where it is even though it is challenging. If you are serious about creating a different life, this book will help you find your way.

My first eye opener was the diagnosis. With that came some realization there was something I could do to correct the problem. I began taking supplements, I already exercised but I got more careful about my diet and protein. I kept looking and eventually found my way to a workshop consisting of the workbook material presented here. This is not a typical self-help book which offers advice on how to change but doesn't show you how. It is also not a workbook that forces you to have flashbacks to an insane past while you do the exercises. We don't use the past, but look to developing the future and the present and look for ways to change.

We have ADD/ADHD (referred to as ADD for the purposes of this book) and that is the way it is. What we are going to do about it is a life choice. I have heard many people blame ADD for all their life problems or troubles: failed marriages, bad upbringing, addiction, violence, etc. Life is how you live it and how you want to get to your goals or objectives not about all the reasons or excuses you have for not getting there. I'm an alcoholic because I have ADD and therefor I am not capable of being anything more. Life is not about finishing in first place and everybody else is a loser. It's about finishing and doing the best that we can as a person, worker, parent, spouse, or citizen.

If we have goals, we have some motivation to achieve or get there and if we have a plan, motivation will be stronger. And when we finish we will have a sense of accomplishment and we will be better, stronger and willing to do that again. Ah, confidence earned makes us want more of that.

It's like eating an elephant, seems impossible but if that is the goal, we start to plan with a manageable idea if we break it down to reasonable amount of one bite at a time. If we can formulate a plan within reason, how do I make it last without going bad, I might come up with storage or a bigger freezer. But first, I should butcher it, can I get help and I could share it. How many ways can I cook this? Anything can be simplified and broken down into manageable chunks. Has finding a solution for ADD seemed impossible, it's not. I have found a way and I have been able to overcome alcoholism and PTSD once I learned how to cope. I have also helped many find a way. ADD is my friend and it has helped me be the person I am today, it has helped me be a good soldier, a good policeman, a good businessman and it continues to help me accomplish goals today as a coach, author, father and spouse. I have also decided I wish to pursue a masters degree in social work.

I don't want to rehash what I already said in the book so, I'll try to present another perspective. I know of a few people whom seem to have this life challenge. I use this term as it is a disease, and it can be challenging but it can be overcome. From the statistics I have read, people are capable of overcoming it if they are willing to put the work into it. I realize that not everyone comes from a shitty past, some can become overwhelmed by the unfamiliar territory of not being able to cope with their demons. How does someone become accustomed to this sort of problem?

My father became an obvious alcoholic in later life, but most of his life I recall, he drank daily at least one double, sometimes more and on weekends perhaps more and at social gatherings even more. He was at times a harmless drunk who preferred to give unsolicited and many times unwanted advice. But he could lay on a pretty good beating. His father had been a sailor for about twenty years in late 1800s, I'm pretty certain he had some of those daily rations of grog. My dad's mother was about four foot eight, but a tyrant. My mother didn't drink but was raised by a tyrant father who had somewhat loose morals, who beat his kids with a whip at times in a drunken stupor and who knows what else. She more or less followed his methods but no whip. I would suggest the idea that I come from a co-dependent family whom also came from a co-dependence upbringing. My older half-brother became an alcoholic in later life and followed the routine of when he was abused, he would kick the dog but he liked the dog so there I was. I also became an alcoholic.

This is one side of the coin, the flip side is the damage that is done to our genes. There is evidence that when our parents drink to excess prior to us being born there is genetic damage done to the genes we get. This has been tracked from grandparents to our parents to us. The damage shows up in the form of ADD or ADHD (I'll call these both ADD for now). ADD has been found or determined to show up in seven different forms with us. Some might get one or two of the traits and some might get six or seven. One of the extra benefits that one might get is anxiety and depression. A common method of coping with the many forms of ADD is using prescription meds which have been known to be misdiagnosed by general practitioners six out of ten times (oops wrong meds). Give Ritalin to an ADHD kid and watch them bounce all over the place (it's a stimulant, they need to calm down). Some just drink, sometimes the booze really compounds problems. I know a kid who came from a straight family, no drinking or drugging, no abuse. He was sniffing gasoline before it was fashionable in the nineteen forties. We have to find ways to cope. The problem here is nobody knows what to do with us, schools fail us, parents don't know how to cope with us, and we can be outcasts amongst our peers.

Here's the problem for those of us whom don't know how to let out our emotions or feelings. We got this sometimes huge vat of bad memories inside of us. Now we get into a bad situation or we witness a bad situation and we don't know how to debrief even under people trained in debriefing grief or bad situations. We can pretend to laugh it off or think it's not that bad but can't get it out of our mind. Our sleep can be fitful or not at all. So, we just add some additional bad memories to our ever growing vat of garbage in our minds and keep trying to cope with whatever methods. A major incident that happens to a child who has ADD is the lack of coping skills and then our inability to cope with PTSD when it occurs and you don't know how to talk about it, you are so screwed.

I have worked with many workbooks when I was trying to fix myself with the help of counselors. The workbooks seem to make me crazier because they tend to freshen the bad memories you might have partially remembered or revived memories you had successfully buried. Now you are reliving all that as well as that most recent event that pushed you to the edge.

We believe that reliving the story or the past is painful and need not be done unnecessarily. If this story of yours has been told at least three times that is enough. There is no relief in telling this story more than that. In fact there isn't relief in telling it over and over. Contrary to telling your story until you get used to it, is like reliving the pain and the memory over each time you tell it. It's called a flashback and this is bad enough when we have them on our own let alone if it is forced upon us, (that is barbaric). Someone who specializes in Neuro Linguistic Programming or in Hypnosis can offer a way of relieving the memory removing the distorted feelings which arise from such an incident, changing the outcome of the incident or some can assist you in removing the memory.

Be cautious in your selection of such a person as like many professions, there are good and other categories.

I like to think in terms of focusing on the future because we have already been living in the past and that is where we usually get stuck. This is a good place to tell you what our objectives will be for this workbook:

To show you how to create a better life for yourself – based on your self-evaluation.

To help you determine whether your current actions and decisions will lead you to the goals or successes you want for yourself.

To help you find better ways to meet your needs.

To help you understand and take responsibility for the choices you make, so you are able to strengthen your relationships through personal change.

To help you self-evaluate symptoms and complaints and change them, to better deal with current relationship problems.

Our major premise is that we as individuals are responsible for our own choices, decisions, goals and the general degree of happiness in our own lives. Through our program, you will come to understand why and how you make the choices that determine the course of your life, recognizing that:

1. You have freedom to make choices.
2. You must take responsibility for your choices.
3. Your behavior should be considered in its totality.
4. Your capacity to change is within you.
5. You are only a victim if you choose to be.

The single most important question to aid your self-evaluation based on today is, based on what I have been doing, "How has that working out for me?" From there, the Dynamic Discovery process will help you change whatever behavior is preventing you from getting or becoming whatever you really want.

Throughout this workbook, you will be asked a number of questions in order to keep you focused on where you want to go, on a daily basis or longer term. Some of these questions:

1. What is my greatest fear in respect to my issue?
2. What do I want?
3. What am I doing to get what I want?
4. Is it working?

I suggest you write out your answers, acknowledge them and then get on with doing something about them. If fear is your greatest weakness and it will always come true if you obsess about it. However, behind your greatest fear or problem lies your greatest strength. Deal with it and become stronger; ignore it and become even weaker.

Once you go through the process we describe here, you will come to realize that the best reason to change your behaviors is to benefit yourself – to make your life better. If you want to be happy, you will have to take responsibility for your life. To do otherwise is to become a victim or codependent.

You can capitalize on this opportunity to start over. All you have to do is say, Enough! As of right now, I'm going to make a new start.

This workbook is not going to take you down memory lane where you can learn to despise me because of the unpleasantness my work may bring to your life. This workbook will get you to look at yourself and what you think, how you behave and how you feel. This might also show you how your body and mind reacts to your methods of coping. The workbook is hard as it will question you constantly but will help you more than anything you have ever worked at. This workbook is designed from a workshop I attended which changed my life or at least helped me along the path in a major way to changing my life for the better. The workbook will challenge you to change the manner in which you think, feel and behave. It helped me make sense of my world which enabled me to look for more steps in the right direction. I owe my life to my friend, George, who took me on this journey to find out what I wanted and that was peace of mind, happiness and enjoyment of my life. I have these things now and I really enjoy my life and everyone and all that is in it. In retrospect I think. I was in hell with my life of negativity, self-pity, victimization, addiction, etc. It wasn't good, it's not that I didn't like my life, I hated it....

Best wishes on this journey out of your hell! There is hope and help.

1

EVERYBODY NEEDS CONTROL

We try to control ourselves, other people, and situations to meet our own needs or to get what we want.

Often we are not aware that we are doing this. We may walk to the shop to buy something we want, but be unaware of our surroundings as we walk down the street. Indeed, we may be 'a million miles away' in our minds, daydreaming about something but still ending up in the shop we wanted to go to; we were able to control our direction and our walking, even though we were not aware of what we were doing!

Everybody needs a certain amount of control to meet their needs for power, belonging, freedom and fun. The most important word to notice here is 'everybody'.

You need a certain amount of control. Your partner needs a certain amount of control. The boss needs a certain amount of control, but so does the worker. The parent needs a certain amount of control, but so does the child. The customer needs a certain amount of control, but so does the shopkeeper.

When people fail to recognize that the other person also has a need for control, the stage is set for conflict. If, however, we are willing to negotiate and compromise, we can find ways to cooperate and create a better life.

Sometimes, we ask for what we want. This respects the sense of control of both parties. (If you don't believe asking is an attempt to gain some control, consider the outrage in the workhouse when Oliver Twist 'asked for more'.) Sometimes instead of asking, we demand what we want. But demanding what we want ignores the other person's sense of control, and they will want to resist us.

Control is all around you. If you're scared to go to work and stay in bed instead, you are controlling your situation, at least to the extent of not going to work. If you buy a lottery ticket, you are trying to exercise a little bit of control over your future, however poor the chances of winning. If you hear there's going to be a gasoline shortage and you hoard gasoline, you are trying to gain a little control over the future. If you boss people around, you are trying to get control over them.

And if they find a way to cheat you or con you, they are trying to get some of their control back.

WHAT WE CAN CONTROL

There are four aspects to everything we do: Thinking, Doing, Feeling and Physiology.

So if you are angry, you may: think 'What a rat such-and-such a person is' (Thinking), kick the dog (Doing), have that burning angry feeling (Feeling), and have adrenalin and other chemicals in your bloodstream (Physiology).

A small change is all that is necessary: A change in one part of the system can affect change in another part of the system. We then have the sense that positive changes will at least continue, and may expand and have beneficial effects in other areas of the person's life.

Of these four aspects, the one that is most in your control to change is Doing. Regardless of how you feel, you almost always have some control over what you do.

Law, morality, politeness and many other human institutions recognize this fact. You may feel angry with me, but you are not entitled to assault me; you are expected to exercise some control over what you do.

The key point to remember about changing what you do is this:

If you do something that is better than what you are doing now, there is a good chance that your thoughts and feelings will also change in a more positive direction, even if change may not come right away.

To put it more simply:

Doing something better than what you are doing now will push your feelings towards the positive.

Again:

Do better to feel better.

Don't wait until you feel good about doing something that might help. If it might help, do it even though you may not feel enthusiastic at the time.

Doing comes first.

First, do better. Then feel better.

When you notice that you are not getting what you want, you need the flexibility to change what you are doing in order to get a different result. The human nervous system can be thought of as goal-seeking, and we tend to get what we focus on, so one of the key questions is 'What do you want?'

Well-formed outcomes are an important tool for ensuring that you get more of what you want in your life. In order to identify where to focus your attention, ask yourself:

What do I currently believe is holding me back from achieving what it is that I really want to achieve?

____

____

____

2

EXAMPLES OF DYNAMIC DISCOVERY LANGUAGE

Human essential needs can be broken into two categories. One is the need to love and be loved at all times during the course of a lifetime. The other is the need to feel worthwhile to one's self and others. In order to feel worthwhile, one must maintain a satisfactory standard of behavior. In other words, if a person is drinking to avoid facing reality, then he or she is not maintaining a satisfactory standard of behavior and not feeling worthwhile. Everyone has these essential needs, but our abilities to fulfill them vary.

The process of fulfilling the essential needs requires, first and foremost, involvement with other people who are in touch with the reality of the world. Without involvement with other people, we try to fulfill the basic needs in unhealthy ways, like overeating or abusing drugs. Not knowing how to fulfill essential needs always leads to pain, either physical or emotional, for the client or those around him or her.

Dynamic Discovery does not concern itself with a client's past. Neither do we deal with unconscious mental processes. We acknowledge distress but focus on success. You will be encouraged – through self-evaluation – to find your own solutions. Different forms of questions enable this process. In these ways, Dynamic Discovery is a very different approach to problem-solving.

Dynamic Discovery tends not to use typical psychology labels – like 'neurotic' or 'dysfunctional' – because these terms tend to stereotype people. Responsibility and irresponsibility are two terms commonly used in Dynamic Discovery:

> Responsibility refers to the ability to fulfill one's needs and to do so in a way that doesn't interfere with someone else fulfilling their needs. For example, responsible students do their

own homework. Dynamic Discovery holds that we learn responsibility through involvement with another responsible person. We can learn and re-learn responsibility at any time in life.

Irresponsible people cannot fulfill their own needs, or they fulfill their needs at the cost of negatively affecting someone else. Irresponsible students look for someone else to do their work. If a parent does the homework for the child, the parent is also being irresponsible. The student who doesn't do their homework is harming their own learning process and being a burden on those around them. The parent who does the homework is harming the student by not teaching that child responsibility.

3

WANTS AND CHOICES

WANTS

There are people who spend all their time getting what they want and they're not happy people. So is there more to Dynamic Discovery than just getting what you want?

We actually ask, "What do you REALLY want?" rather than simply "What do you want?" Let's elaborate on this.

A man goes into a DIY shop and asks for a paintbrush. "What do you want to do?" asks the lady behind the counter. "I want to paint my car," replies the customer. "Maybe a can of spray paint is what you want," suggests the shop lady.

The moral is... if this man had received what he wanted, would he have gotten what he really wanted – which presumably was a reasonably presentable car (spray-painted) rather than a streaky one (brush-painted)?

People come to us with all sorts of problems, but these problems might be classified into three (often overlapping) situational types:

1. My picture does not meet my needs (although it is easy enough to achieve in Behavior).
2. I cannot make my picture happen (i.e., translate into Behavior, although it would be need-satisfying).
3. The inner logic of my picture has problems.

An example of Situation 1 is the picture of drugs. I can get drugs easily enough, but ultimately they do not meet my needs (although I only put them into my picture album in the first place because they appear to meet them).

An example of Situation 2 is where I know that the picture of joining the local choir is need-satisfying, but I am too shy to approach the club premises. I lack the skills or knowledge to make my picture happen in the real world of Behavior.

Situation 3 is directly relevant to this discussion about wants. The paintbrush, for example, appears to be what I want, but there is a flaw in my logic, in the way I connect my pictures together. Paintbrushes are simply not for painting cars!

The way people handle (or generally mishandle) time management is full of examples of logic breakdowns.

Many people come to the Dynamic Discovery program because their lives are messing up, in spite of apparently getting what they want. In a sense, they have all the paintbrushes they have ever asked for and they wonder why they are still unhappy. In the Dynamic Discovery world, happiness is first getting what you NEED before focusing on what you want! In your daily life, you hope that what you want will ultimately get you what you need, but sometimes you get it wrong.

One important theme in Dynamic Discovery is self-evaluating the effectiveness of your current wants:

If you had what you want, would you be happy? (Yes) ___ (No) ___

Is this what you really want? (Yes) ___ (No) ___

How much do you know about what you want?

____

____

Do you also want the consequences of what you want? (Yes) ___ (No) ___

How many years, or lifetimes, will it take you to get what you want right now?

____

____

FOLLOW-UP QUESTIONS

What is one task you have been putting off – a task that you fear doing – even though you know that by completing it you will free up your time and mind?

How would completing this task improve the quality of your life?

In actual workshops, there is a question about Dynamic Discovery that is posed in various ways by group members:

> Are the people you are referring to getting material things or things such as better relationships, marriages, peace, more time? I know many people who have all the possessions they want, but are miserable or feel a void. I also know people who have opted out of ownership to a simpler lifestyle to gain more control over their lives.

Our answer is:

> We are motivated to get what we want. We feel frustration when there is a gap between what we want and what we are getting. For as long as we are alive and kicking, there will always be that gap between what we want and what we are getting, because there is always a new want or situation. So what matters is how we manage that gap between what we have and what we want. Some things we can move towards more effectively; some we must learn to accept less of than we would like, and some we need to take out of our wants altogether or push them way back in the queue. In many ways, Dynamic Discovery is about how we manage that frustration and what we do with it.

To say that people are motivated by what they want is not the same thing as saying that getting what they want will inevitably 'make' people happy. A lot of Dynamic Discovery is about negotiating the conflicts between your wants and those of others, or between contradictory wants you might have. Sometimes it's the way in which people go about getting what they want that makes trouble for them.

"Happiness is not getting what you want, but wanting what you have."

Rabbi Hyman Schachtel

While that quote is somewhat of a twist of how we understand 'want' in Dynamic Discovery as it directs our Behavior, it provides a powerful insight as to how to address many of the realities of our lives.

It seems that after we secure one want, goal, etc. we are on to the next. What I may see as a desire to continually improve, others may see as perpetual dissatisfaction.

Dynamic Discovery makes a distinction between our Needs (survival, love and belonging, achievement/power/recognition, fun, and freedom) and our Wants (which are the pictures we have in our head as to how to satisfy those needs). Our wants or pictures change as to how to best fulfill our needs because we change. As a child, my picture of fun was playing ball with my friends. As an adult, my picture has changed to going to a movie or having friends over for dinner. With new information, experiences, etc. we look for different ways to satisfy our needs. Without changing wants, we remain static – with no life mission or growth. It is true that what you see as a way to improve, others may see as perpetual dissatisfaction. That's because they are looking at the world through their perception of life, with their own pictures and wants as to how to best get their needs met. Fortunately, it is not through their perception that you must live your life, but through your own.

You can move yourself towards what you want by self-evaluating how your life is currently to allow you to determine where you really want to go, and the key to getting there is to write it out in detail. Follow these steps to get you started on your journey:

1. State your goal in positive terms: What do I want?

____

____

2. Self-evaluate your goal: Am I doing this for myself or someone else?

____

____

____

____

Does my goal depend solely on me?

(Yes) ___ (No) ___

3. Define your goal: Where, when, how, and with whom do I want it?

4. Describe the details of the process:

What will I be doing to get my goal?

What will I see, hear, and feel when I have it?

5. Identify the resources you need.

What resources do I have now?

What resources do I need to acquire?

Have I ever achieved this goal – or something like it – before?

What happens if I act 'as if' I already have it?

6. Is your goal ecological – that is, without direct sexual competition? (Yes) __ (No) __

What is the real purpose behind why I want this goal?

____

____

What will I lose or gain if I have it?

____

____

What will and won't happen if I get it?

____

____

What will and won't happen if I don't get it?

____

____

7. Describe the first step you will take toward achieving your goal.

____

____

If you are struggling with one or more or all of the above, there is a way to clarify. You may have never really thought about what you want or what you might be capable of, because you may be so focused on your daily routine that you just haven't taken the time to think about your own future. Suppose somebody said you could have anything you wanted in the world – anything at all – how would you know what to choose? What would you do if you knew you could not fail? Write out your answer:

____

____

____

____

____

Think about what would happen if you actually succeeded at Doing whatever you wrote above. Most people doing this exercise find that they start off with some conventional answer almost automatically – but when they have had some time to actually absorb the idea of being unable to fail, they come up with an entirely different, and sometimes surprising, answer. Your answer will tell you what you really want to achieve.

Write out your answer to:

'What would happen if you succeeded?'

____

____

CHOICES

Choice is not totally avoidable. We cannot choose not to choose! It has been noted many times by many behavioral professionals that doing nothing is still a choice – and that is only one of the realities that we deal with in Dynamic Discovery. The inevitability of choice is not a limitation. It is within our power to make some change in our own lives. The following notes suggest a structure for learning to deal with the unavoidable choice. Needless to say, they should not be followed in a cookbook fashion.

What is the problem? Although it sometimes takes a lot of time, there is a critical point in Dynamic Discovery when you will become aware of how your life differs from your ideal world; how what you have is not the same as what you want. The more specific this awareness, the better. This process requires that the problem area be identified already.

What are the OPTIONS open to you? To answer that question, you can ask yourself:

What do I want?

____

What is that going to do for me?

____

What's stopping me?

____

What's important to me here?

____

What's working well?

___

___

What resources are going to support me?

___

The above questions may help you identify one or more approaches to dealing with the problem. Depending on the seriousness and complexity of the problem, it may be necessary to extend the list of options by consulting outside experts.

However, you should always ensure that one option describes a 'no change' scenario. This is the 'zero option'. It can also be helpful to include possibilities that appear far-fetched or even funny.

Establish the INEVITABILITY OF CHOICE. Sometimes it can be useful to get you thinking of choice by remarking to yourself, "When I leave here, I can choose to leave things as they are. I can choose the 'no change' angle or I can opt for one of the other plans.

I cannot foresee the future, but good planning depends heavily on good anticipation. That's the best I can do."

Answer the following questions:

1. Is it possible not to choose? (Yes) ___ (No) ___

2. What do I think of having a closer look at each of the options before I choose?

___

What are the possible CONSEQUENCES of each of these options? Here, you question each option on your list:

3. What do I think might happen if I chose this option?

___

4. If I choose this, what else am I probably choosing?

___

___

___

5. How might I feel once I make this choice?

____

____

____

6 What would be good about it for me and what would be bad about it?

____

____

____

7. How certain can I be about these outcomes?

____

____

____

How do you EVALUATE each of these options, bearing in mind their consequences? If you could award a satisfaction rating to each of these options where the maximum score is 100%, what would you give to each option? This will help you compare the options and make an evaluation of each.

Which CHOICE will you take? Maybe all your scores are between 90% and 100%, but even if they are between 10% and 15%, you still have a choice and you can pick whichever seems best or whichever is least bad. You may think you have no choice when none of the available choices score well. Writing down the different options and giving each a score can help you see that, no matter how bad they may be, some choices are better than others.

How can you PLAN to make that choice a successful reality? This has to do with planning and rehearsing. Look at plans for carrying out this choice. Do you need to learn new skills? Why not practice them now?

Making the best choices to satisfy your needs applies in any environment, no matter how restrictive or impoverished.

All choices occur within boundaries. If you're in a city and you want to go out tonight, you have a myriad of choices. The boundaries to those choices will include legal restrictions, financial restrictions, other people's rules and so on, but essentially you have hundreds, if not thousands, of choices. If you're living in a refugee camp, the boundaries are much tighter. If you're locked in a room, they are tighter still. So while you will almost always have choices, they occur within boundaries.

Sometimes these boundaries are such that all the choices are painful. A child in an orphanage who's locked into the boiler room for the night has choices (curl up, bang on the door, try to sleep, etc.) but they are terribly constricted by the boundaries imposed by whoever used their power to throw them in there. They are also painful choices. People often have to choose between painful alternatives because that's all that is available. There is also the question of 'choices' which are made so fast that we are not aware of making them.

Choices are part of everyday life, no matter what situation we are in.

Our approach is to say something like "we understand that in the past you may have been a victim and you may feel like a victim now, but you can choose to see this placement at the group home as punishment or an opportunity to stop your mind from bouncing, and assess where you are and move ahead. You can choose to run away (explore consequences here – more restrictive placement, jail) or you can choose to accept some of the help that is available – school, job counseling, activities that may get you to your community or home faster."

Finally, look at your Behavior. Is your Behavior getting you closer to home or further away?

ATTITUDE AND EMPOWERMENT

The longer I live, the more I realize the impact of attitude on life. Attitude, to me, is more important than facts. It is more important than the past, than education, than money, than circumstances, than failures, than successes, than what other people think or say or do. It is more important than appearance, giftedness or skill. It will make or break an organization or a home.

The remarkable thing is you have a choice every day regarding the attitude you will embrace for that day. You cannot change your past, and you cannot change the fact that people will act a certain way. You cannot change the inevitable. The only thing you can do is to play on the one string you have, and that is your attitude.

I am convinced that life is 10% what happens to us and 90% how we react to it. And so it is with you – we are in charge of our attitudes.

In Dynamic Discovery, the emphasis on choices (in attitudes and actions) is empowering, and can be very liberating – but we need to realize that the available choices can be restricted by other people, the weather, etc.

You have choices about how you feel in a given situation, and that how we feel will often be most easily influenced by the control you take over your Total Behavior – particularly your actions and thoughts.

Sometimes you may choose to feel sad because feeling sad is an appropriate response for you to your life circumstances at a particular time; e.g. when that circumstance is sad and the response is to grieve. How you choose to behave in terms of your actions and thoughts will govern how you may gradually come to resolve a difficult issue for yourself. For example, if you were grieving or otherwise choosing to feel sad or depressed, you could choose to drink alcohol, take drugs, sleep all day, isolate yourself from others, think that life is not worthwhile or that you have a bad 'lot' in life, etc., etc... or you could choose to seek support from a counselor or good friend or family member, get some exercise, seek small enjoyments in life, think that you will overcome this bad period, and so on.

Where 'Attitude' comes in is that you need to take on the attitude that you are in control of your life, and that how you act and think is your easiest route to altering how you feel. Attitude should not involve just 'getting on' with things in spite of emotional pain, because people need to recognize their pain, seek assistance to help them deal with it, have it validated – at least validate it themselves – but then make positive choices to help them deal with the issues.

It's important not to confuse thinking with feeling. You have the most control over what you do, and more control over what you think than what you feel. Therein lies the power of positive thinking.

Let that sink in ...

What you think and do has total influence over how you feel.

Everything can be taken from you but one thing: The last of your human freedoms – to choose one's attitude in any given set of circumstances. Choices are always available. Conditions may make some choices less desirable and change the nature of the choice, but it's still there. If you plan a picnic and it rains on that day, you can still have your picnic, but you have to choose to have it indoors or choose to get wet. The choices are not restricted, but their impact has changed.

Your attitude is a choice, much like other choices.

For instance, an individual may be experiencing grief issues over the loss of a loved one and, out of need, he convinces himself that he has to take on an attitude of nonchalance. This may help him to deal with his grief for the moment, but not in the long run. If, however, he believes that 90% of life is about how he reacts to it, he may take on an 'attitude' of 'I can handle it'. Rather than dealing with and working through the trauma, he instead deals with it only on the surface. With counseling – if he gets counseling – he may be enlightened on how attitude is important but can be overstated, and he may come to realize that attitude is not the be-all and end-all coping tool.

With Dynamic Discovery, you will learn how to make the changes that put your problems where they belong: behind you.

Automatic choices or forgotten choices are still choices. It is important to remember that you are always responsible. You may make a routine choice and do not put much thought into it, but you are still responsible. The example of driving a car and being a million miles away in your mind is a great example. After all, if by being a million miles away you got into an accident, then you are responsible for that choice even though you did not mean to make it. That consequence may make you more aware next time.

Some of what we do is genetically encoded and in that sense, perhaps it is done at a subconscious level.

Are those 'choices' we make outside our awareness really choices at all, or are they automatic actions or forgotten choices or actions taken while we are asleep (in the sense of not being aware of what is going on)? This is important because so much of life involves routines carried out beyond our awareness (like driving a car while we are elsewhere in our minds), and when we describe these as choices, we seem to 'blame' those who carried out these actions.

Sometimes we cannot choose the development of politics, social changes, etc. that force us to be in awkward situations. But when someone is in a certain situation – such as being a refugee or an orphan, or being abused, etc. – they still have choices they can make, such as living a dignified life, submitting to the authorities, accepting the fact of not having parents, etc.

You can make choices in any immediate situation which could make a great difference to your ultimate quality of life.

Being truly present in the moment includes an immediate consciousness of every choice, which requires the highest process of reasoning and thinking.

Consider the following ...

- Everything you do or have is the result of the choices you make.
- You will always experience what you create (through your choices).

1. What is a decision you know you need to make and you have put off?

____

____

2. What action would you have to take in order to achieve your outcome?

____

____

3. What is the potential risk of taking this position?

____

____

4. How will it feel to have accomplished this action?

____

____

EMPOWERMENT

Dynamic Discovery is not about being presented with a good dose of reality or harshly being told to get on with things. It is more to do with helping you to self-evaluate in order to find better ways of meeting your needs and taking responsibility for yourself and your life.

Once the basics for survival – food, clothing and shelter – are catered to, humans have other more complex psychological needs – such as the need to love and be loved; the need to belong; the need for power, self-worth, freedom, and happiness. Each of us has these needs but some need more of one thing than another, and what makes it harder is that often you are not actually aware of exactly what it is that you need.

Dynamic Discovery is used to bring about change while respecting the needs of others. Learning to assess one's needs and to alter one's life, in small but

positive ways to fulfill those needs, is a significant step towards progress and ultimately taking responsibility for one's own life.

In Dynamic Discovery, our basic human needs are classified under five headings:

- Power – which includes achievement and recognition; feeling worthwhile;
- Love and belonging – which includes groups as well as families or loved ones;
- Freedom – including independence, autonomy or your own space;
- Fun – including pleasure and enjoyment;
- Survival – nourishment, shelter and reproduction.

One of the core principles of Dynamic Discovery is that, whether we are aware of it or not, we are always acting to meet these needs, but not necessarily in an effective manner.

Socializing with people is an effective way to meet our need for belonging. Sitting in a corner and crying in the hope that people will come to us is generally an ineffective way of meeting that need – it may work, but it is painful and carries a terribly high price for ourselves and others.

If life is unsatisfactory or we are distressed or in trouble, we need to check whether we are succeeding in meeting our basic psychological needs for power, belonging, freedom and fun.

Because we're alive and functioning, the survival need is normally being met. It is in how we meet the other four psychological needs that we run into trouble.

To check out whether you are meeting your needs, the three basic questions that are asked are:

1. What do you want?

____

2. What are you doing to get what you want?

____

____

____

3. Is it working? (Yes) ___ (No) ___

Then it's time to make workable plans to get what you want. Consider the following:

4. If you had a magic potion that allowed you to wake up tomorrow with everything you ever wanted in your life, how would your life be different?

____

____

____

5. What would your life consist of?

____

____

____

____

Dynamic Discovery has to be about things that are in your control – things that are possible to do.

For instance, maybe you can't make your spouse talk to you, but you can talk to them; maybe you can't get your teenage son to treat you with respect, but you can decide that you will no longer provide a laundry and catering service to a son who treats you with contempt; you can't make the company give you a promotion but you can look for it, lobby for it and apply for the job when it comes up.

Dynamic Discovery will empower you by emphasizing the power of doing what is in your control to do. In Dynamic Discovery, changing what we do is the key approach to changing how we feel and to getting what we want.

Control is also very important. Our focus is on individual choices and sticking to what is within our own control to do, while respecting other people's rights to meet their own needs.

In Dynamic Discovery, we delve into the past but not to a great extent. The past is seen as the source of individual wants and the origins of ways of Behavior, but there are both good and bad things there. Our emphasis is on learning from the past but focusing on the present and empowering individuals to satisfy their needs and wants now and in the future.

It is very much a process of hope, based on the conviction that we are products of the past but we do not have to go on being its victims.

4

TOTAL BEHAVIOR AND CHANGE

As human beings, we have many needs – which can be grouped under five headings:

1. Love and Belonging
2. Achievement, Power and Recognition
3. Freedom
4. Fun (enjoyment, appreciation)
5. Survival (and safety)

When our life is out of balance, we can look at these needs and assess whether one or more of them is being frustrated. If so, we can focus on things we can do – that are within our control – to bring about a better balance. These do not have to be major things. Here is a list of the major needs, and examples of how we might meet them:

LOVE AND BELONGING

Giving and receiving love and/or sex; being part of something; belonging to groups; having or being someone to talk to; receiving attention; sharing experiences; supporting teams, political parties; working; chatting; greeting.

ACHIEVEMENT, POWER AND RECOGNITION

Visualizing what you would be doing, thinking, and feeling if your self-esteem was strong and positive; what it would look like to feel powerful, achieving, and worthwhile; to 'see' yourself as competitive, confident, and a 'winner'.

FREEDOM

Space; spreading my wings; elbow room; time to myself; independence; autonomy.

FUN

Enjoyment; pleasure; appreciation; laughter; games, learning.

SURVIVAL

Food; clothing; shelter; health.

If life is unsatisfactory, if we're distressed or in trouble, a quick check of whether we're meeting our four basic LAFF needs (the fifth, Survival, is implied)is in order, because it's often in an attempt to meet those needs that we run into trouble.

CHECKING IN WITH YOURSELF TO STAY ON TRACK

Whether we are aware of it or not, we are all the time acting to meet our LAFF needs. But we don't necessarily act effectively.

So, in order to keep on track to where you want to get, use the following checklist of questions to ask yourself:

1. What do I want?

___

2. What is that going to do for me?

___

3. What's stopping me?

___

4. What's important to me here?

___

5. What's working well?

____

6. What can be better?

____

7. What resources are going to support me?

____

THE KEY IS WHAT WE WANT

Nobody ever gets up in the morning and says, "I must meet my Love and Belonging need today." We are more likely to say something along the lines of, "I wonder if Mary is free for lunch today" or "Maybe we can get the gang together on Friday night." We want to have lunch with Mary or to marry John or to go out with our pals on Friday night or we want 'our' football team or 'our' political party to win.

So what really drives us as social beings is our wants. We don't think of our needs as such. We think of what we want, behave to get what we want, fantasize about what we want and so on.

As well, asking yourself (and others) questions with the appropriate structure and voice tone can help change your state and focus.

DEFINE YOUR QUESTION

Instead of asking yourself "Why am I lazy?", ask yourself "How can I change my state so that I become energetic?" If your brain does not come up with an immediate answer, then ask with intensity and expectation and you will eventually advance in that direction.

DIFFERENCES

There are many ways to meet your needs. We can think of the things we want as ways of meeting our needs – effectively or ineffectively.

We all need to eat, but I want a steak and you want a pizza. Not only do our wants often differ, but the details of our wants are very specific. I want a sirloin steak, cooked medium, in a black pepper sauce; you want a deep-filled ham and mushroom pizza with no peppers. I want a socialist government that will pay for social services for people on low incomes; you want a capitalist government that will cut welfare and taxes. To the extent that we can respect the fact that other people – including those nearest and dearest to us – want different things than we want, we can live in harmony. If we cannot respect these differences, then we must live in conflict.

To get what we want, we behave. We are engaging in one Behavior or another from the time we are born to the time we die. But this Behavior has components, and when these are put together, we can think of them as constituting Total Behavior.

TOTAL BEHAVIOR

At any time, four things are happening for you: what you are doing, what you are thinking, what you are feeling, and what is going on in your body.

Sometimes these activities work in harmony. For instance, if you are pleased, you may be smiling (doing), thinking positive thoughts, feeling content, and physically relaxed. If you are angry, you may be shouting (doing), thinking angry thoughts, feeling that you are in a rage, have your heart beating quickly and your muscles tensed up.

Often, the four activities are going in different directions. If you are sitting in a dentist's waiting room and you hear the drill starting up, your feelings may tell you to run but your thinking may tell you to stay. Your body may be tensed up with heart racing and adrenaline pumping. And you may be idly thumbing through an out-of-date copy of Hello! magazine.

You could say that at any one time, we are behaving in each of these four ways: feeling, thinking, doing, physiology. We can call this combination our Total Behavior. If we can change one of these behaviors, then we have a good chance of changing the others.

A small change is all that is necessary. A change in one part of your system can affect change in another part of your system, and you may have the sense that positive changes will at least continue and may expand and have beneficial effects in other areas of your life.

It is hard to change our feelings directly. It is easier to change what we are thinking, and easiest of all to change what we are doing.

So the golden rule is: if you want to change how you feel, begin by changing what you are doing or what you are thinking. Easy to say and hard to do? Yes! Let's look at it a little more closely.

CHANGING HOW YOU FEEL

Consider the four components of Behavior: Doing, Thinking, Feeling, Physiology. Which do you focus on moment-to-moment?

You always know how you feel, but if feelings are your moment-to-moment guide to what to do next, you may be in difficulty; if you feel angry, you may lash out at someone or you may become depressed to suppress the anger.

Moreover, if there is something you need to do, you may make the mistake of waiting until you feel right about it before you do it. Suppose there's an important phone call you have to make but which you never actually 'feel' like making when the time comes to do it. If you are led – on a moment-to-moment basis – by how you feel, there is a good chance you will never make the call or that you will postpone it until you are in trouble and cannot put it off any longer.

But you can change your focus so that you are purpose-led instead of feelings-led. You are still very aware of your feelings – they are the warm, beating heart of your life – but your purpose is your moment-to-moment guide and your orientation is towards doing.

So now you make your telephone call, even though you don't feel like making it at this particular moment. With the phone call made, you – hopefully – feel relief, a return of energy – perhaps even a little elation.

Paradoxically, by focusing on what you can do rather than on what you feel, you arrive at a point where your feelings become pleasant and positive.

Another example: if you feel tired and tense and stressed and you go for a brisk, 10-minute walk – even though you don't feel like it – you are likely to have more energy and to be in a better mood afterwards. Here you have done something (gone for a walk) which has changed your physiology (increased energy), and now you feel better.

Sometimes the good feeling takes longer to arrive. If you are grieving over the end of a relationship or over a death, you will – hopefully – get to the point where you are doing things you want to do – seeing friends, taking a break and so on – but it may be a long time before this 'feels' right and before you start to feel good. But you will get there, if you have the courage to keep working at it – and it will help greatly if you have friends to help you along the way.

This raises an important point about the things you want. Sometimes you cannot move ahead unless you change what you want.

Suppose you want the renewal of a relationship more than anything else, but you know it simply isn't going to happen. For a time, part of the pain you feel comes from wanting something you can never have or can never have again. This wanting and this pain is part of grieving. In time, you must come to wanting somebody or something else in place of what you have lost. If you persist in wanting the person you have lost, you must be prepared to reduce the importance of that want to you – you must allow other wants to take priority.

Here are five questions (and statements) to help expedite your self-evaluation process:

1. What have I been doing to solve my problem(s)?

Begin by looking at what you have been doing to solve the problem

___

___

___

2. How is what I'm doing helping me get what I want?

It might be helpful to think about your behavior to see how each method is working for you.

___

___

___

3. What might be some other things I could try?

You could look at some new ideas to try when you are ready to look at moving toward a plan for meaningful change

___

___

___

4. Which idea would I like to try first?

You can identify several possibilities. Write out what you think about trying any of them

___

___

___

___

5. When?

Figure out when to talk about whether your plan is working

____

____

6. Then ask, "What is in it for me? What is in my best interest?"

____

____

____

This approach is geared toward taking the steps needed to put you on track to finding better ways to meet your needs. Just as the essence of life is building loving relationships and a solid career or other meaningful activities that contribute to society, the essence of Dynamic Discovery is building and maintaining relationships and improving home, social and work performance to meet one's basic needs.

So in order to bring about change in your life, you must do something different or change what you want. If you want to be a good athlete but you spend your mornings in bed, you must change what you do – get up and start running instead of snoozing – or change what you want – perhaps decide that what you really want out of life is to be a couch potato.

Notice that doing something different involves a change in thinking. Instead of thinking, "I must have this," you decide (and making the decision is also a form of thinking) that "I will settle for that."

DEFINE YOUR QUESTIONS

Instead of asking yourself "Why am I lazy?" ask yourself "How can I change my state so that I become energetic?" If your brain does not come up with an immediate answer, then ask with intensity and expectation – and you will eventually advance in that direction.

Your thoughts are somewhat under your control. They wander off on their own every few minutes (if not every few seconds!), but you need to be willing to change what you think in order to change what you do. Sometimes, however, your emotions are so strong – with grief or depression, for instance – that all you can change is what you do, and even your thoughts have to follow afterwards.

Bear in mind that when you want what you've never had, you must do what you've never done. Change allows that to happen.

5

CONFLICT IN RELATIONSHIPS

The two major personality types are extroverts (also referred to as extraverts) and introverts. These are opposite ends of the spectrum of personality traits. Extroverts and introverts become friends and/or fall in love all the time – because opposites attract – but may find it difficult to build a strong relationship or marriage because of communication differences.

Though relationship conflict is inevitable, resolving conflict and improving communication is easier when you understand introverted and extroverted personality types.

There are eight personality types anchored by two temperaments – introversion and extroversion – which creates 16 personality styles. Under those two umbrellas, there are four different functions: feeling, thinking, sensing and intuition.

Noted psychologist Carl Jung believed that introverts draw energy from their inside world. They take time to observe situations and determine a viable course of action before jumping in. Extroverts, on the other hand, look to the outside world for energy. They thrive in social situations and tend to be more outspoken than their more reserved counterparts.

According to an article posted on PsychologyToday.com, these differences may in fact be hardwired into a person's biology. In a 2009 study, PET scans were utilized to measure cerebral blood flow in both introverted and extroverted individuals. The researchers noted that there was increased activity in the frontal lobe in introverts while extroverts experienced increased blood flow to the back of the brain.

One is not better than the other, just different.

The only person any of us can change is ourselves, and we will only change if it makes sense to us and gets us something we want. For instance, an angry person will only work to learn how to cope/manage/deal with their anger when it makes sense to them. We do not willingly change for others, but we do change for our own reasons. This is because all human Behavior is deliberate and purposeful and intended to achieve something or get us something we want – whether it works or not.

BEHAVIORS

So, why do we humans do certain things, act certain ways, when that particular Behavior seems to not work? The simple answer is memory. Nearly everything we do is dictated by memory. When we smell something, we automatically check our memory bank to determine whether the smell has been experienced before. If it has been, we have the solution to the question. If it hasn't, we then have an unanswered question. If we find the answer to that question – maybe by asking someone else – we have one more 'fact' in our memory banks. If we do not answer the question, we still have a memory of a smell that is simple unlabeled.

Whenever we meet someone, we scan our memory to determine whether we've met that person before and, if so, what they mean to us. If they are strangers, we determine who they remind us of and what that person meant to us. Based on memory, we form instant judgments. It's not about right or wrong, good or bad, strong or weak; it's all about memory. AND FEELINGS.

A person who uses arrogance or anger or snideness – to the extent that many or most people do not want to be in their company – is likely doing it because at least one time it worked, or appeared to work, for them. A memory is created such that the mind asks "What do we do when we feel like this?" and the answer is, "We act arrogant/angry/snide" and so we do – long after it quits working.

Why do you do the things you do? Because you want to. And you want to because that's what you've learned to do. And you believe you're right and anyone who disagrees with you is wrong. You have to feel that way because your perception is your reality. If you believe it to be true then it is true – for you!

The solution to any human problem is always simple, but seldom easy. Never confuse simple with easy. The solution to any addiction is to simply cease the addictive Behavior, but if it was an easy thing to do, then far more addicts would discard their addictive Behavior. Even amongst those addicts who do work at overcoming their addiction, some 85% relapse – because overcoming is NOT easy.

What is a decision you know you need to make and you have put off making?

____

____

6

CHOICES AND DEPRESSION

In Dynamic Discovery, depression is seen as a way of dealing with the gulf between what we have and what we want. Because depression is seen in this way, we always hold out for the possibility of overcoming depression. And, as is clear below, Dynamic Discovery does not see depression as being bad all the time. Sometimes it is better than the alternatives.

What is important is not to trap ourselves in depression. What is more important is to know that the path out of depression begins with changing what we want or changing how we behave.

Depression can do four things for us – and knowing what these are can help us to begin the climb out into the light. These four things can be thought of under the acronym ACHE.

A FOR ANGER

Depression is often considered an alternative to anger, and sometimes it can be better to choose depression than anger. If you make a habit of lashing out when anything goes wrong, you can alienate other people and often make matters worse. Consider how many relationships anger has destroyed. Consider how many lives anger has destroyed. Anger has its place, and it often gives us the energy for change, or the energy to stand up for ourselves. But it can be destructive, too. Depression can be a safe, temporary alternative to anger. It becomes unsafe when it goes on for too long or we use it too readily.

C FOR CONTROL

Depression gives us a certain amount of control over people and situations. It may help us to avoid taking risks, to stay in a safe environment. To a certain extent, people will try to avoid upsetting us when we are depressed. If we are absolutely devastated by something that has happened, depression may give us the only control over our lives that we can handle at the time. The price for this control, of course, is very high – because of the suffering that comes with depression. By definition, nobody enjoys depression – if we did, it would not be depression.

H FOR HELP

Depression brings us a certain amount of help. This may be help from friends, from a doctor or from an institution. Some people need this help for a time. Again, if it goes on too long, people may stop helping us and, in any event, depression is a high price to pay for the help we get. But why don't we just ask for help? For many of us, it isn't such an easy thing to do, to say "I am in a bad way; please help me." Many of us have the tendency, when asked "What's wrong?" to reply, "Nothing," – even though there may be a great deal wrong. Depression can get us help without us having to ask for it.

E FOR EXCUSE

Depression can excuse us for not doing what we should do. It can be a way of avoiding pain. If I am depressed, how can I be expected to get out and about, dress well, work, face my problems, etc.? Yet, very often, it is only by doing these things – even, at an extreme, by doing something, anything at all – that I can start to climb out of a depression.

So, if I am depressed, Dynamic Discovery would say that I can begin to climb out of the depression by taking action.

I have no direct control over the feeling of depression. I may, if I am in the depths of depression, have little or no control over my thoughts. All I can control is what I do. Maybe all I can do is get out of bed and sit by the window, or get out of bed and go downstairs.

When I can do a little more, I should try to do something more. Ideally, I should focus on small things that I want and that I can get.

Maybe I want my children back living with me, but I can't get that because they've grown up and flown the nest – but maybe I can telephone or write to them. Maybe I can spend more time with my friends or more time doing something else that I want to do and that is unattainable.

I also need to change what I want – in this case, to accept that my children will never return to live with me.

Is this easy? No. Sometimes it's very difficult and takes a long time. Our feelings, thoughts and actions are linked, but sometimes we have to do something for quite a long time before our feelings follow and become positive.

Although this work can be slow (though it isn't always slow) it's worth the effort. Injunctions to "snap out of it" and to "pull yourself together" are often ineffective. If we could snap out of it, we would. The work of changing our

Behavior even while our feelings remain low will be far more effective in the long run.

MEDICATION AND DEPRESSION

Many people have a great deal to say about medication, but I do not have the qualifications to discuss it, and my attitude is that I have nothing useful to contribute on the topic. But I believe that, whether you are on medication or not, Dynamic Discovery can make your life better.

BEHAVIOR

The 'Behavioral Car' is a way of illustrating a key aspect of Dynamic Discovery: imagine that our Total Behavior is like a front-wheel drive car in which the two wheels at the back represent Feeling and Physiology and the two front wheels represent Doing and Thinking. It is by changing the direction of the two front wheels that we change the direction of the car. In other words, to change how you feel, change what you do and/or what you are thinking.

Sometimes people who are attending a therapist say, "I've got depression. What are you going to do about it?" And their therapist will just as often reply, "I know what you mean. I'll get back to you on it." But they seldom do.

However, Dynamic Discovery is a most useful tool for anyone who wishes to cease depressing and choose a more positive Behavior. Unfortunately, orthodox medicine tends to most often stuff people with drugs. To be fair, they don't rule out counseling altogether, but claim that a patient with severe depression needs to have the individual's chemical imbalance corrected before they are able to benefit from counseling.

I have had occasion to meet up with people who will not – for their own reasons – take medication but wish to stop depressing. Under such circumstances, I explain the Control Car and how, through Dynamic Discovery, they might be able to deal with depression – if that's what they really want.

Orthodox medicine holds that people are depressed because of a chemical imbalance – and, to me, that is like saying a man was running because he was sweating. In each case, the chemical imbalance and the sweat are the physiological component of the Total Behaviors chosen to depress and to run.

All cases are, of course, different, but it is better to do something rather than nothing, and it is better to do something enjoyable rather than just 'do'. That is to say it is better to walk up and down than just sit, and it is better to go out for a walk with the dog or play tennis or whatever turns you on than just walk up and down.

The principle of tiny bites also applies. If you feel you cannot manage a long walk, how about around the back yard or to the end of the block?

Look at your problem through the following six questions:

1. What?

____

2. Which?

____

3. Who?

____

4. When?

____

5. Where?

____

6. Why?

____

____

'Why?' is the only question that doesn't ask for specific detail. The answer to 'Why?' is usually 'Because...' and a historical or theoretical explanation. You may get specific detail in response to 'Why?', but that will only be a lucky accident. In Dynamic Discovery, we seldom ask 'Why?' – instead relying on the other five questions.

Much attention has been focused on how to overcome depression, but it is often forgotten that it is not always wrong to depress. Most of us depress three or four times a day. It is often a wise choice: it is wiser than anger, which could have physical consequences. Often we need time to withdraw; bereavement is an obvious example. Depressing here and there is quite legitimate. It is only when the Behavior continues and no longer provides effective control that it needs to be addressed.

The point is that it is a choice.

IMPORTANT NOTE

The foregoing discussions about conflict and behaviors and choices make clear that we are governed by our nature (personality) and perceptions – all of which are merely reflections of our Values and Beliefs systems, which are important because:

- Our beliefs become our thoughts
- Our thoughts become our words
- Our words become our habits
- Our habits become our values
- Our values become our destiny

THE 'SHOULD' QUESTION EXERCISE

Divide a sheet of paper into three columns. At the top of the first column, write the words 'I Should...'

Then in that column, write down all the things that you feel you should be doing. The list can be as long or as short as you like.

Look at your list and rearrange them into the order of 'most important'. Then beside each 'I Should...' statement, ask yourself 'Why?' and write down the answer in the second column.

Then for each 'I Should...' statement, ask yourself 'Says Who?' and write the answer in the third column.

This exercise helps you to find the basic beliefs you have about yourself. The 'Says Who?' column will challenge your assumptions and show how you have been programmed to believe certain things that are causing problems for you. For example:

I SHOULD...

Find a different job

Become more aggressive

WHY?

To earn more money

To take control of situations

SAYS WHO?

My Wife

My mother

Now go through your list again, but this time rewrite all statements as 'I Could...' These will turn into your affirmations. These affirmations will target the things in your life that you may want to focus on.

For those of you who are really 'stuck' because of your 'limiting' Values and Beliefs, you will find a free downloadable workbook (What Are Your Values?) on our website (www.DynamicDiscovery.ca) that was specially devised to provide a concise, systematic way to change those Values and Beliefs that are interfering with your ability to be happy.

7

INTRODUCTIONS

In actual workshop (group) situations, everyone in the group is introduced the same way, through asking the key questions to elicit information about what individual group members want, and to begin evaluations of what they have been doing in order to achieve those wants. You can use the same process to work on your own wants.

If the answers do not come easily to you, please be aware that most people give little thought to what they want or what they might be capable of, because they are so focused on their daily routines that they just don't take the time to think about their own future – which is the route to a wasted life. This is your opportunity to use our process to answer the 'want' question.

KEY QUESTIONS

1. What has been going on that led you to (or back to) Dynamic Discovery?

____

____

____

2. What have you done to try to resolve your problems?

____

____

3. How did it work out? Did it help you get what you want?

---

4. What do you want?

---

5. If you got that, what would it mean to you?

It may appear that our method of questioning ignores a lot of important information. The overall goal during the introductory session is to find out what you want and if your current and past behaviors are pertinent to moving you toward that goal. This exercise is for you to identify what you really want so that you are able to make a start at getting what you want and need – regardless of past behaviors – to find solutions to the areas of challenge for you.

The fact that you have been taking action to try and change your life is encouraging, but those actions may not help get what you really want. The problem lies not with your willingness to change or to work for change, but with your inability to find an effective means of doing so.

If your answer to Question #5 above – directly or indirectly – was that you wanted 'to be happy', then we can help you get started with that. However, if your answer was somewhat – or a whole lot – less than 'happy', then I would invite you to go back and work through all five questions again – because we have found that when clients describe the feeling or sensation they seek from getting their wants satisfied, none of them want anything less than happiness, peace, contentment and strength. Because happiness can mean a whole list of things, and it will be helpful if you develop your own list of definitions.

If you are finding it difficult to determine what you really want, just utilize the following process which may provide an answer for you:

Suppose somebody said you could have anything you wanted in the world, anything at all, how would you know what to choose?

One way is to ask yourself "What would I do if I knew I could not fail?" and note your answer.

Think about what would happen if you actually succeeded at achieving your answer. Most people who do this exercise find that they start off with some conventional answer almost automatically, but when they have had some time to actually absorb the idea of being unable to fail, they come up with an entirely different – and sometimes surprising – answer. Your answer will tell you what you really want to achieve.

____

____

____

____

In a group situation, it is at this point that the group members realize they all want basically the same things, regardless of how different they may be as individuals. They are able to identify with their common wants – which is taking a positive approach.

8

FEELINGS

For Dynamic Discovery purposes, we want to deal with emotional feelings, not the physical aspect of feelings. Just trying to feel better doesn't work; although we try and try to change our world by trying to feel better, nothing changes.

We also deal with conscience and guilt as two separate emotions. We define conscience as the emotional hotplate which allows us to evaluate our personal interest in an issue. Conscience, upon understanding, is that feeling of deep regret. Guilt is when we don't like or want the feeling we get from an action, but we do the action anyway. Administering through guilt is difficult, because we all understand guilt differently and apply it differently.

If administering through guilt worked, we would only have to use it once to get others to change their behaviors. In the case of a child being told that their behavior causes pain to Mommy and/or Daddy, that pain is not real to them and they can't relate to it. If, however, their conscience allows them to remember the pain they felt from a behavior, then they can find value in changing that behavior.

Experiential learning has more value than theoretical learning because of the mind's ability to memorize the thoughts, feelings and actions associated with the learning.

The question to address is: 'What kinds of feelings have you been struggling with just prior to your decision to enroll in Dynamic Discovery?' At this point, you should make a list of all the feelings that you have been having problems with, both now and over the course of your life. (Do this on the lines below.) Not limiting the feelings to current feelings takes the focus away from today and removes any confessional tone to the discussion, and offers you a chance to honestly self-evaluate these feelings without fear of being criticized or judged.

Now name a feeling you have had sometime in your life that you did not like having. This is a feeling that did not help you get what you wanted. It may be a feeling you are struggling with right now, but it doesn't have to be.

You likely don't find it difficult to describe the past feelings that have caused you the most disruption and discomfort in your life. You can describe these feelings as "unwanted."

KEY QUESTIONS

(Please note that we are only dealing with feelings at this time and you should check to see if any of your responses are thoughts instead of feelings.)

1. What feelings have you had in your life that you didn't like?

(For a list of unwanted feelings compiled from actual group sessions, see Page 145)

2. How many hours a day are you dealing with feelings you don't like?

____

____

____

____

3. Which of the feelings on your list have you not felt?

____

____

____

____

4. Are your feelings the biggest problem you have? In other words, if you could somehow feel better, would things be 'alright'? (Yes) ___ (No) ___

5. How would you like to be feeling?

(For a list of wanted feelings compiled from actual group sessions, see Page 145.)

____

____

____

____

It is possible for you to start feeling these emotions if you are interested.

The choice is yours. You must decide.

Your road to ongoing recovery could involve the challenge of reaching for the feelings you want to be experiencing.

DISCUSSION OF FEAR AS THE ROOT OF OUR UNWANTED FEELINGS

In group sessions, when we write out our list of unwanted feelings, the word FEAR is listed on the board in capital letters to denote its importance in our lives. Having established how seriously these feelings have affected the lives of the group members, we move into a discussion on FEAR.

We talk of the nature of fear, with the natural 'fight or flight' response. You likely understand that fight or flight responses occur over the short term, but you may not have considered the phenomenon of living with these sensations over an entire lifetime.

In an actual group session, asking the group members to define FEAR is usually unproductive – often producing only silence – so we provide the dictionary definition: 'a distressing emotion aroused by impending danger, evil or pain'. This definition implies that FEAR is a simple response to a threat. When our needs are not getting met, we experience FEAR.

At this point, the question to the group members is, "Do you want to have FEAR?" The answer is always, "NO!" The next question is, "Do you want to be able to respond to a threat?" The answer here is always, "YES!" We don't dwell on this discussion, except to make the point that FEAR is merely a response to a threat. The threat does not have to appear real to anyone other than the person experiencing the FEAR. The point is made that it is a very smart system that perceives a threat and responds to it.

Fear is the 'driving' feeling behind all other unwanted feelings and is the root of guilt, anger, and so on. As a group, we discuss the fear that is contained in the other feelings on the list, like getting caught in the feeling of guilt. Quite often, the group likes to deny any fear in guilt, so they are asked a hypothetical question: "When you meet someone whom you like and who obviously likes you, do you ever think that this person won't like you once they get to know you?" There is usually general agreement.

What is your answer to that question?

(Yes) ___ (No) ___

In an actual workshop, we go through some of the feelings on the list that the group creates, and we talk about what fears pertain to the unwanted feelings. Anger is a feeling that can easily hide the fear factor. Very often, people who are angry in no way appear to be full of fear. However, if we accept fear as a simple response to a threat, we can see the fear in an angry person. Many people who use anger as a continuous controlling Behavior are simply using a purposeful and selective Behavior for trying to meet their needs.

Using the consistent questioning approach, the connection to fear is made in each and every instance. This moment in the session is often a turning point for the group members.

If you're struggling with a fear, you can use a visualization exercise to test your connection to fear. Essentially, you go through the memory of an experience of a traumatic situation so as to be merely watching the event and not re-experiencing it.

Make sure that you're in an environment where you feel safe and secure.

1. Identify the traumatic or unpleasant memory that you want to diminish.
2. Remember that you were safe before and after the unpleasant experience.
3. Imagine yourself sitting in front of your television set and watching yourself on the screen – in black-and-white only.
4. Now imagine floating out of your chair, out of yourself – and as you float and hover, you can see yourself sitting in your chair and watching the black-and-white film of you on the television screen.
5. Still in black-and-white on the television screen, imagine running the film back to before you experienced the memory you want to diminish and running it through until after the experience when you were safe.
6. Now freeze the film or turn the screen completely white.
7. Now imagine yourself floating into the end of the film.
8. Run the film backwards very quickly – in full color – as if you're experiencing the film, right back to the beginning, when you were safe.
9. Repeat steps 7 and 8 until you're comfortable with the experience.
10. Now go into the future and test yourself against the diminished memory of the once-powerful and fearful memory.

DEFINING LOVE FOR OUR PURPOSES

"ONE WORD FREES US OF ALL THE WEIGHT AND PAIN OF LIFE: THAT WORD IS LOVE."

SOPHOCLES

Love refers to a variety of different feelings, states, and attitudes that ranges from interpersonal affection ("I love my mother") to pleasure ("I loved that meal"). It can refer to an emotion of a strong attraction and personal attachment. It can also be a virtue representing human kindness, compassion, and affection – 'the unselfish loyal and benevolent concern for the good of another'. It may also describe compassionate and affectionate actions towards other humans, oneself or animals.

Love may be understood as a function to keep human beings together against menaces and to facilitate the continuation of the species.

There is an old saw that says there is a thin line between love and hate – therefore, love is giving someone the power to destroy you, and trusting them not to.

A dispassionate description of 'love' is the scientific one: Recent studies in neuroscience have indicated that as people fall in love, the brain consistently releases a certain set of chemicals, including the neurotransmitter hormones dopamine, norepinephrine, and serotonin, the same compounds released by amphetamine, stimulating the brain's pleasure center and leading to side effects such as increased heart rate, loss of appetite and sleep, and an intense feeling of excitement. Research has indicated that this stage generally lasts from one and a half to three years.

ENDNOTE: Love can make you do anything and sacrifice for what will be better in the end. Love is intense and passionate. Everything seems brighter, happier and more wonderful when you're in love. If you find it, don't let it go.

THINKING

"WE CAN'T SOLVE OUR PROBLEMS USING THE SAME KIND OF THINKING WE USED WHEN WE CREATED THEM."

ALBERT EINSTEIN

This is where you investigate the connection between thinking and feeling, and how you can change the way you feel by changing your thinking.

This is not about trying to better your thinking, or making you a better person. The idea is for you to make changes in your thinking behavior so you can think about yourself exactly how you want to think about yourself.

Usually, we cannot shut off our thinking – we can only think about something else.

In relationships, we can get along if we can find out what we like about others and what we want from the relationship. If we can make some connection – no matter how tenuous – we can use it as a foundation to build on.

Is Dynamic Discovery nonsense because it is just words?

Well, words are all we have that we can rely on, because everything in our life starts with a thought – and our thoughts are only our unspoken words.

All human relationships require communication. When communication ceases, the relationship stops growing and often dies. Words are all we have that we can rely on.

KEY QUESTIONS

1. What have you been thinking that you don't like? Or what have you been thinking that has not helped you get what you want?

(For a list of unwanted thoughts compiled during actual group sessions, see Page 145.)

____

____

2. Have you ever thought you were stupid, a failure, etc. after something you've done?

   (Yes) ___ (No) ___

3. If this is what you were thinking, how would you expect to feel?

____

____

4. If you were happy, what would you be thinking?

____

____

5. What could you do to start thinking that way?

____

____

____

An exercise described in the book shows the connection between the 'feeling' and 'thinking' behaviors. Everyone is asked to close their eyes and do the following, one step at a time, pausing for about 30 seconds to perform each task. To do this exercise on your own, make yourself comfortable and follow the instructions:

1. Think of the color red.
2. Think of the color blue.
3. Think of the color yellow.
4. Be sad.

5. Be happy.
6. Open your eyes and raise your right hand.

The object of the exercise is to show you that you can make a conscious decision to change your thoughts and feelings.

Self-evaluate the exercise by asking yourself "*What did I do when I thought of the colors (red, blue, yellow)*?" and *"What did I do to feel happy and sad?"*

How did you do it? Write your answers here:

____

____

____

____

If you were unable to visualize ('see') the colors or feel the emotions, it's okay – because you will be able to make the exercise work for you by closing your eyes and asking yourself "What if I could see the colors and feel happy then sad? What would the colors and the emotions 'look' like?"

Write your answers on the lines above.

The next discussion relates to 'secret' (destructive) thinking, and I recommend that you refer back for this discussion.

NOTE: This session is not about trying to better your thinking. Nor it is about making you a better person. The goal is to make changes in your thinking behavior, so that you can be thinking about yourself in a way that is exactly how you want to think of yourself.

9

ACTIONS

All behavior is deliberate and purposeful. We choose behaviors in an attempt to meet our needs, or to get what we want. Even if the behavior we choose does not get us what we want, we will continue to choose it until we learn another behavior.

Drinking/drugging is a behavior – a response to a need – that is purposeful and need-fulfilling. Although alcoholism is a disease – it meets the definition of a disease by being chronic, progressive, incurable and potentially fatal – the alcoholic still has the choice over taking the first drink. There can be both an addictive and a behavior component to drinking/drugging, but one can be a heavy user without being an addict. The behavior component is when we use drugs/food/exercise/etc. to avoid, replace, remove or forget our problems.

We cannot have an action without a thought. Our thoughts are often so fast that we are not fully conscious of them – but try to walk or talk or swing your arm without thinking. To hit someone 'without thinking' would seem improbable unless you can make your arm swing without giving any thought to the action. Try it.

Although there is such a thing as involuntary/reflex actions, they usually occur in bizarre circumstances. Instinct, such as flight and fight, still requires some thoughtful direction, but it may be limited to focusing narrowly on the problem at hand.

Changing what we do is the key to changing how we feel and to getting what we want.

Sometimes we are so caught up in anger, depression or resentment that even changing how we think seems an impossible task. In such situations, a positive change in what we do may be the best we can manage.

KEY QUESTIONS

1. What have you been doing that you do not like doing? Or that has not helped you get what you want?

(For a list of unwanted actions compiled during actual group sessions, see Page 145)

____

____

____

____

____

2. Which of the actions on the list have you not done?

____

____

____

____

____

3. What do you want to be doing?

(For a list of wanted actions compiled during actual group sessions, see Page 145)

____

____

____

____

____

Emotions are a wonderful, immediate and 'alive' source of information about how we are doing and whether we are happy with what is going on in our lives. But it is very, very hard to change our emotions directly. It is easier to change our thinking – to decide, for example, that we will no longer think of ourselves as victims or to decide that in our thoughts, we will concentrate on what we can do rather than what we think everybody else ought to do.

However, there are times that we are so caught up in anger, depression or resentment that even changing how we think seems an impossible task. In such situations, a positive change in what we do may be the best we can manage.

Remember this: Changing what we do is the key to changing how we feel and to getting what we want.

These five questions (and statements) help expedite the self-evaluation process to put you on track to finding better ways to meet your needs:

1. What have you been doing to solve your problem(s)?

____

____

____

2. How is what you are doing helping you get what you want?

It might be helpful to think about your behavior to see how each method is working for you.

____

____

____

3. What might be some other things you could try?

We could look at some new ideas to try when you are ready to look at moving toward a plan.

____

____

____

____

4. Which idea would you like to try first?

You have several possibilities. Write out what you think about trying any of them.

____

____

5. When?

Figure out when to talk about whether your plan is working.

____

____

____

____

____

6. Then ask, "What is in it for me? What is in my best interest?"

____

____

____

____

____

In psychology, it is assumed that people have certain basic needs – and in Dynamic Discovery, they are classified under five headings for which we apply the acronym LAFFS:

1. Love and Belonging – this includes sex, families or loved ones, as well as groups.
2. Achievement, Power and Recognition – which includes feeling worthwhile as well as winning.
3. Freedom – includes independence, autonomy, your own 'space'.
4. Fun – includes pleasure and enjoyment.
5. Survival – includes nourishment and shelter.

Whether we are aware of it or not, we are always acting to meet these needs, but we don't necessarily act effectively. Socializing with people is an effective way to meet our need for belonging. Isolating and self-pitying in the hope that people will come to us is generally an ineffective way of meeting that need; it is painful and costly (in psychological terms) and seems to never work in the long-term.

So if life is unsatisfactory, or we are distressed or in trouble, one basic thing to check is whether we are succeeding in meeting the first four of our five basic psychological needs – only those four because the fifth (survival) is implied – because it is in how we meet those four 'psychological' needs that we run into trouble.

THE KEY IS TO KNOW WHAT WE WANT

It is not usual to think in terms of meeting our Love and Belonging needs each day as we are more likely to wonder whether a friend would be able to meet us for lunch or to consider getting a group together for a social evening. We may want to meet a friend or mingle with a group or want 'our' football team or 'our' political party to win.

What usually drives us as social beings is our wants, since we don't think of our needs as such. We think of what we want, behave to get what we want, fantasize about what we want and so on. We can check whether we are meeting our wants through addressing three basic questions:

1. What do I want?

____

____

2. What am I doing to get what I want?

____

____

3. Is it working?

____

____

____

PLANNING

In order to get what we want, we need to make a plan that is workable – meaning that it is a plan we can successfully implement. In other words, it concentrates on the things that are within our control to do:

- You may not be able to make your spouse talk to you, but you can talk to your spouse.
- You may not be able to make your teenage son treat you with respect, but you can decide that you will no longer provide a laundry and catering service to a son who treats you with contempt.

- You may not be able to make the company give you a promotion, but you can look for a promotion, lobby for it and apply for the job when it comes up.

In answer to the above points and further to the three questions above those points, here are four more questions:

1. Is what I'm doing helping me get what I want? (Yes) ___ (No) ___

2. If not, what might be some other things I could try?

____

____

____

3. Which am I most likely to try first?

____

____

____

4. When will I start?

____

____

____

There are four aspects to everything we do: Thinking, Doing, Feeling and Physiology. So if I am angry, I may think what a rat such-and-such a person is (Thinking), kick the dog (Doing), have that burning angry feeling (Feeling) and have adrenalin and other chemicals in my bloodstream (Physiology). (Again, change the examples to have more effect on the client.)

Take a minute and let that sink in …

Of these four aspects, the one that is most in our control to change is what we do. Regardless of how we feel, we almost always have some control over what we do.

Law, morality, politeness and many other human institutions recognize this fact. You may feel angry with me but you are not entitled to assault me. You are expected to exercise some control over what you do.

The key point to remember about changing what we do is this:

If you do something that is better than what you are doing now, there is a good chance that your thoughts and feelings will also change in a more positive direction, even though the change may not come straight away.

To put it more simply:

Doing something better than you are doing now will push your feelings towards the positive.

To put it more simply again:

Do better to feel better.

Don't wait until you feel good about doing something that might help. If it might help, do it even though you may not feel enthusiastic at that time.

Doing comes first. First do better; then feel better. In this way, we are empowered by focusing on the power of doing what is within our control to do.

The issue of control is also of great importance.

10

CONTROL

We are a total behavioral system. The human body is a very smart system that has never been fully duplicated. No other living thing has the power of thought and implementation that a human has, nor the ability for change and correction.

First, there is a thought, which is followed by feelings, actions, and physiological response. The system always behaves. A major elevation in any of the behaviors will generally unbalance the system and take us away from where we really want to go.

As part of meeting our needs, we need control: one person seeks control through position and money; another wants to control his or her physical space, like the teenager who bans all parents and parent-like persons from her room; another wants to chair the committee; another wants an office with a corner and two windows; another wants a specific meal on the table at a specific time.

Control gets us into trouble in two primary ways: when we try to control other people, and when we use drugs and alcohol to give us a false sense of control. At the very heart is the idea that the only person you can really control is yourself. If you think you can control others, you are moving in the direction of frustration. If you think others can control you (and so are to blame for all that goes on in your life), you tend to do nothing and again head for frustration.

There may indeed be things that 'happen' to us and for which we are not personally responsible, but we can choose what we do about these things. Trying to control other people is a losing game; a never-ending battle that alienates us from others and causes endless pain and frustration.

This is why it is vital to stick to what is in our own control to do and to respect the right of other people to meet their needs.

We can, of course, get an instant sense of control from alcohol and some other drugs. Unfortunately, our lives are never more out of control than when we are drunk or drugged. There are very few people in this world who ever woke up with a hangover to find that they had fewer problems than they had when they started using the night before.

Excessive drinking and the use of drugs have to be replaced by doing something else – and that something else has to have a fair chance of getting us what we want in life.

We try to control ourselves, people and situations to meet our needs or to get what we want.

Often we are not aware that we are doing this. We may walk to the shop to buy something we want but be unaware of our surroundings as we walk down the street. Indeed, we may be 'a million miles away' in our minds, daydreaming about something but still end up in the shop we wanted to go to; we were able to control our direction and our walking even though we were not aware of what we were doing!

Everybody needs a certain amount of control to meet their needs for power, belonging, freedom and fun. The most important word to notice here is 'everybody'.

You need a certain amount of control. Your partner needs a certain amount of control. The boss needs a certain amount of control, but so does the worker. The parent needs a certain amount of control, but so does the child. The customer needs a certain amount of control, but so does the shopkeeper.

When people fail to recognize that the other person also has a need for control, the stage is set for conflict. If, however, we are willing to negotiate and compromise, we can find ways to co-operate and create a better life.

Sometimes we ask for what we want. This respects the sense of control of both parties. (If you don't believe asking is an attempt to gain some control, consider the outrage in the workhouse when Oliver Twist asked for more.) Sometimes instead of asking, we demand what we want. But demanding what we want ignores the other person's sense of control – and they will want to resist us.

CONTROL IS ALL AROUND YOU. FOR EXAMPLE:

- If you're scared to go to work and stay in bed instead, you're controlling your situation at least to the extent of not going to work.
- If you buy a lottery ticket, you are trying to exercise a little bit of control over your future, however poor the chances of winning.

- If you hear there's going to be a gasoline shortage and you hoard gasoline, you're trying to gain a little control over the future.
- If you boss people around, you are trying to get control over them.
- And if they find a way to cheat you or con you, they are trying to get some of their control back.

KEY CONCEPTS OF CONTROL:

1. All we ever do is behave (good or bad).
2. We are externally motivated by the world around us.
3. If we are sad, unhappy or depressed, it is because we choose to feel and behave that way.
4. We are not victims of our past unless we choose to be.
5. We are constantly seeking to live in our 'ideal' world.

The ideal world is your personal Shangri-La – the ideal of what you want your life to be. It fulfills your most basic needs by placing the actual people you want to love in your ideal world. If you have no one in your ideal world or are experiencing conflict between your ideal world and their 'real' world, there is an approach for that – if you can accept that there is not one 'right' way to view things. Different views may be just as valid and may fit the facts just as well. Views that keep you stuck are simply not useful.

Sometimes all that is necessary to initiate significant change is a shift in your perception of the situation (which is the value of a group setting – more and different perspectives).

Focus on what is possible and changeable rather than what is impossible and intractable. Focus on aspects of your situation that seem most changeable.

- To create a solution to your problem, it is best if you can believe that you do not have to analyze a problem in order to solve it. Indeed, focusing on the problem may actually be unhelpful because your focus can become an obsession from which you cannot divert your attention (the elephant in the living room).
- Start from a premise that you have all the strengths and qualities you need to solve your difficulties – it is simply a question of effectively mobilizing them.

If we control acting and thinking, then feeling and physiology will follow. We choose our behaviors. The only behavior an individual can control is his or her own.

CONTROL CAR

We are a total behavioral system. No other living thing has the power of thought and implementation that a human has, nor the ability for change and correction.

First, there is a thought – which is followed by feelings, actions, and physiological response. The system always behaves. A major elevation in any of the behaviors will generally unbalance the system and take us away from where we really want to go.

The human body is a smart system that's never been fully duplicated in nature. No other living thing has the power of thought and implementation that a human has, nor the ability for change or correction. A front-wheel drive car, like the one pictured below, with well-balanced 'tires', will drive us properly in the direction we want to go. First there's a thought which is followed by feelings, actions and physiological response.

BALANCED EXAMPLE

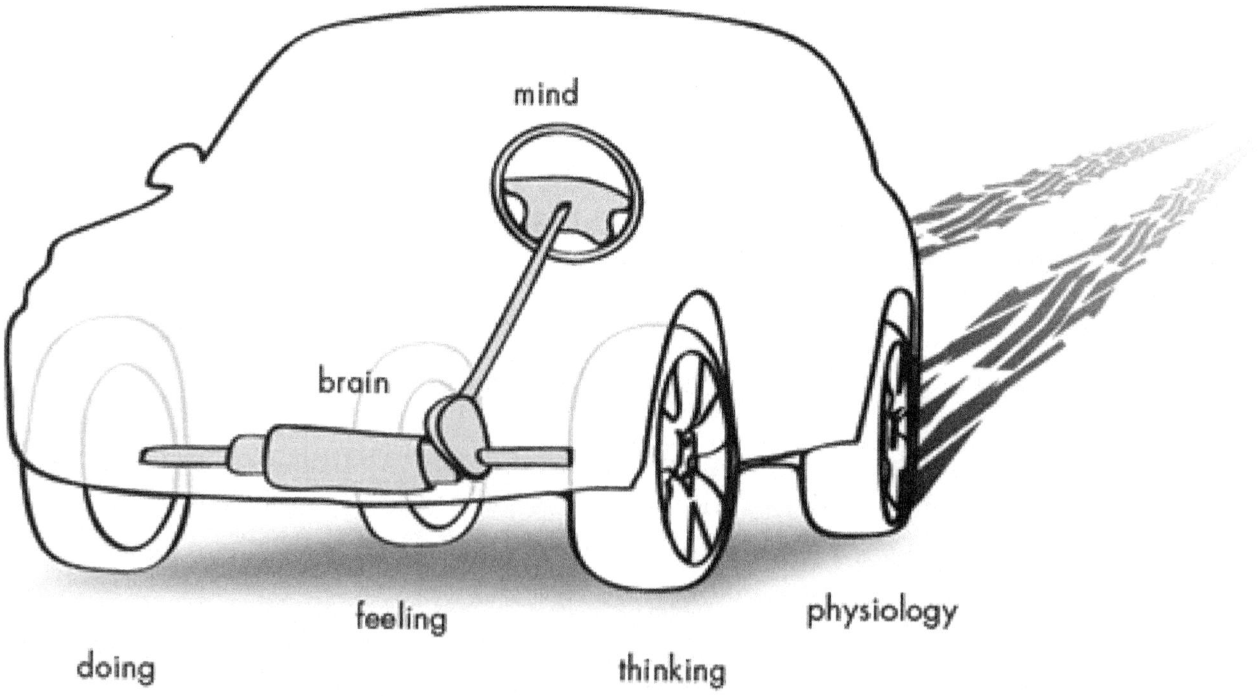

Any major elevation in one or more of our Behaviors would have the same effect as greatly over-inflating a particular tire. Similarly, repression of our Behaviors has the same effect as deflating a particular tire. Either way, it'll cause us to feel 'unbalanced'.

AN UNBALANCED EXAMPLE (SHOWN BELOW)

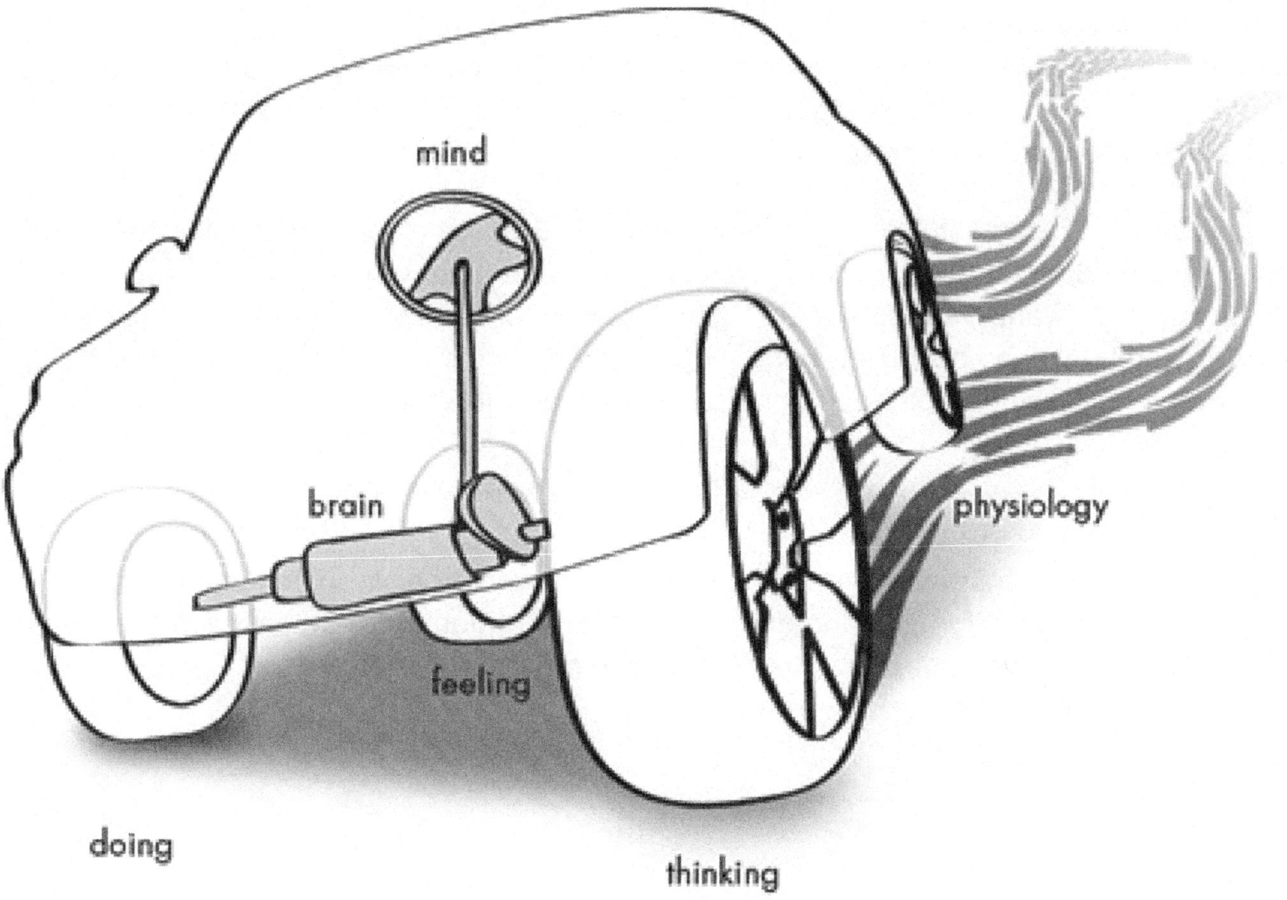

In the example shown on the other page, the thinking 'tire' is obsessive (greatly inflated), the feelings are 'somewhat' inflated, and the actions are 'somewhat' deflated (becomes less active). Done long enough and your health (physiology) could suffer. This car would not steer well – it would not be taking you in the direction you want to go.

CONTROL COMPUTER

The way to change how we feel and what we do is to change our thinking with a new program. The old program and everything we ever learned will always be with us, but we can access the new program and evaluate it for applicability in whatever situation we are in. If we think that the old ways had some value, we can always call them up and evaluate how they actually worked by applying our memory/conscience – or by implementing the actual behavior again.

Using the computer analogy allows us to slow our response time and fully evaluate a behavior prior to implementation.

THEORY

The Control Computer theory illustrates how we can change our thinking to change our lives.

Computer manufacturers mimic the way the human mind works by using us as the model for their products. The human mind is very smart, and the way computers query and sort information somewhat mirrors the human ability for change and correction. The way to change how we think is by trying out a new 'program'.

Since all change is stressful, it is comforting to know that the old program will always be in our memory (or hard drive) allowing us the choice between old and new Behaviors (or programs). If, at any time we want to revisit our old Behaviors we just have to access our memory and take a look. In addition, if the new Behaviors are too extreme we can replace them with another new program – totally new or a blend of our old Behavior and the new.

COMPUTER

In the illustration on the next page, the keyboard represents our thoughts and the monitor represents our mind which forms judgments. A computer's 'judgments' are saved in the memory of one or more drives, while ours are saved in our minds' memory. By hitting 'Print', the computer performs an action attached to the thought.

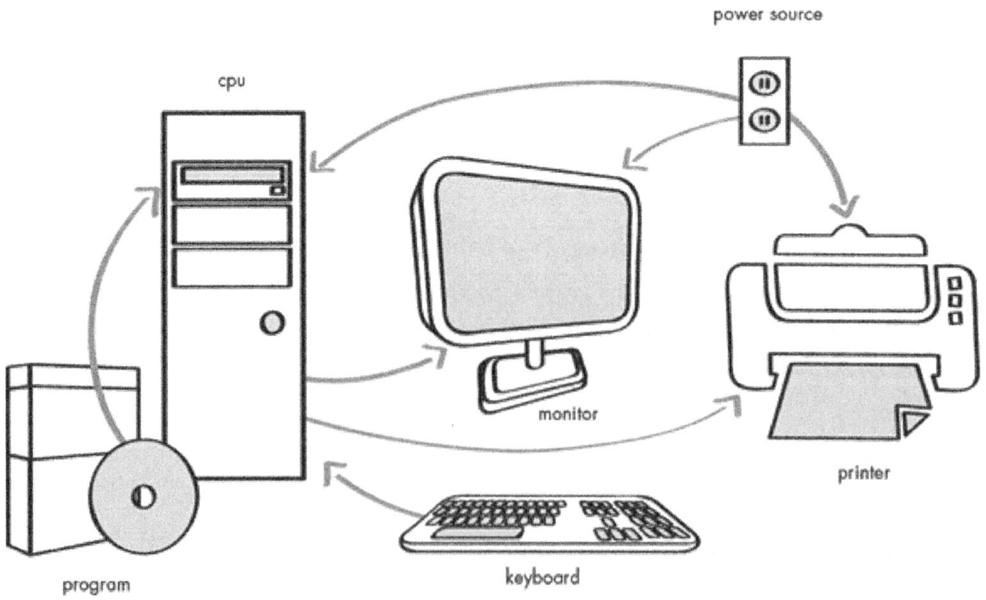

The major difference between the human mind and a computer is that the human mind has the ability to create concepts, whereas a computer can only deal with information that it has.

Let that sink in ...

If we think about a problem that has no readily available answer because we haven't experienced it before, our human mind will come up with outlandish and crazy search results we have no business paying attention to.

A computer can be programmed to make projections, but it does not spontaneously create concepts. To your mind, perception is reality. In many instances, if your mind can conceive it, your body will follow.

The function of the conscious mind is to take in information. The subconscious mind takes responsibility for filing and retrieving that information, and for weighing it against your Values and Beliefs systems. The new information is strengthened or diluted depending on whether it matches your Values and Beliefs systems.

The subconscious mind exists to serve us and will try to find a way for us to get what we want – sometimes to our own detriment. For example:

A person sits on the edge of their bed, ready for sleep, and thinks, "Well, I suppose I'll toss and turn all night, and not get any sleep." Their subconscious will do everything it can to oblige them by interrupting their sleep.

Or prior to going to sleep, they consider some unpleasant things they're scheduled to do the next day. They think, "Man, tomorrow will probably be a really terrible day." Their subconscious will do everything it can to oblige them by putting them in a sour mood.

A computer, when asked to find information that it doesn't have, will search its files and then provide a message advising that the information was not found, and asking whether you want it to continue searching. We must then select one of two options – 'Continue searching' or 'Cancel'.

The human mind, on the other hand – when asked to find information that it does not have – will search and search and search to no end. It does not provide a message asking whether you want it to continue or cancel, and its ability to create concepts can provide some very interesting results. For example:

A person is seriously troubled by a financial problem, and they have no training or experience in solving this type of problem. Their mind will search for solutions that do not exist. They're obsessed – because this problem really offends their Values and Beliefs – so they think and think, and think. At some point, they may ask themselves, "What's going to happen if I can't solve this serious financial problem?" Their mind might take this as an instruction to create a concept, and the concept may create a picture of the person ending up living on the street and eating out of garbage bins – their life ruined, a disgrace. If that's not bad enough, their body will react to that concept, or perception, as though it was real.

A person has been threatened with extreme physical violence by someone they're afraid of.

They have no experience in dealing with a situation like this. They think and think about what to do, and no answer appears. Their mind creates a concept whereby every noise in the house represents someone breaking in, and they see an intruder in every shadow. At some point, the stress will drive them into total collapse – even if the threat was never, ever, actually carried out.

A person who is afraid of the dark is locked in a room with no light source. Within a period of time, they will begin to imagine terrifying presences. Although in reality, nothing is there – their bodies react as though the concept is real.

Let that sink in …

To the human mind, perception is reality. In many instances, if our mind can conceive it, our mind and body can achieve it – regardless of whether the concept is helpful or hurtful.

The subconscious part of your mind is the storage area which holds all of the information that you've accumulated throughout your lifetime – every experience, everything you've seen, heard, felt, smelled, touched and experienced. And it's all filed away as message units sorted into message clusters, or topics.

If you were a computer, your subconscious mind would be the hard drive. Your conscious mind would be the RAM (random access memory), and your Values and Beliefs systems would be the program.

The major difference between the human mind and a computer is that the human mind has the ability to create concepts, whereas a computer can only deal with information it has within its programs.

11

PHYSIOLOGY AND TOTAL BEHAVIOR

At any time, four things are happening for us: what we are doing, what we are thinking, what we are feeling, and what is going on in our bodies – and sometimes these activities work in harmony. For instance, if we are pleased, we may be smiling (doing), thinking positive thoughts, feeling content and physically relaxed. If we are angry, we may be shouting (doing), thinking angry thoughts, feeling that we are in a rage, and having our hearts beat quickly and our muscles tensed up.

Often, the four activities are going in different directions. If you are sitting in a dentist's waiting room and you hear the drill starting up, your feelings may tell you to run but your thinking may tell you to stay. Your body may be tensed up with heart racing and adrenaline pumping. And what you are doing may be thumbing idly through an out-of-date copy of Time magazine… and appearing calm, cool and collected.

You could say that at any one time, we are behaving in each of these four ways: feeling, thinking, doing, physiology. We can call this combination our Total Behavior. If we can change one of these, then we have a good chance of changing the others.

It is hard to change our feelings directly. It is easier to change what we are thinking, and easiest of all to change what we are doing.

So the golden rule is: if you want to change how you feel, begin by changing what you are doing or what you are thinking. Easy to say and hard to do? Yes! Let's look at it a little more closely by briefly reviewing what we have already learned.

CHANGE

Although the four components of Behavior are Doing, Thinking, Feeling, and Physiology, it is best if you are purpose-led instead of feelings-led. You are still very aware of your feelings – they are the warm, beating heart of your life – but your purpose is your moment-to-moment guide and your orientation is towards thinking and doing.

By focusing on what you can do rather than on what you feel, you arrive at a point where your feelings become pleasant and positive – but sometimes you cannot move ahead unless you change what you want.

Let that sink in …

In order to bring about change in your life, you must do something different or change what you want – and that involves a change in thinking or doing. However, if your emotions are running wild – with grief or depression, for instance – it would not be unusual that all you can change is what you do … and then your thoughts, like your feelings and physiology, have to follow.

KEY QUESTIONS

1. In what ways have activities that you haven't liked doing affected your physiology?

____

____

____

2. How would your life look if things were the way you wanted?

____

____

____

3. What is something you can do to help you get what you want?

____

____

____

12

BEHAVIOR AND RELATIONSHIPS

The surest way to bring people into your circle (closer to you) may be to attract them in through behavior changes.

If Self = Best Interest, then who is the best person to look after your best interest?

For Dynamic Discovery purposes, best interest is defined as not being deliberately hurtful or harmful to self or others.

> You operate as a 'smart system' that is capable of evaluating for your needs and determining what to do in order to meet those needs. Once you build your library of activities and events that will help you meet your needs, your 'smart system' will evaluate and choose the best option(s).
>
> Because no other person can live your life for you, it follows that you are the one person on this planet who can restore your own dignity and self-respect. No one else can do that for you.

KEY QUESTIONS

1. How has your behavior affected your relationships?

___

___

___

2. What are your best interests, and where are you in relation to them?

ACTIVITIES

1. Diagram your relationships as affected by your behavior. (relationship circles)

This is an example of one client's 'Ideal World':

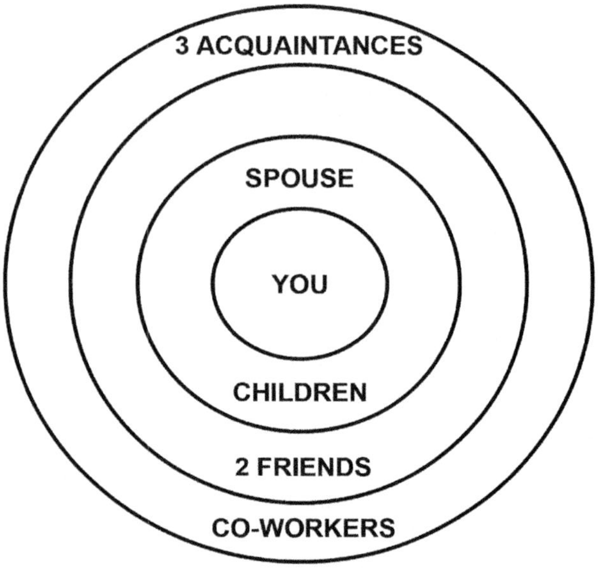

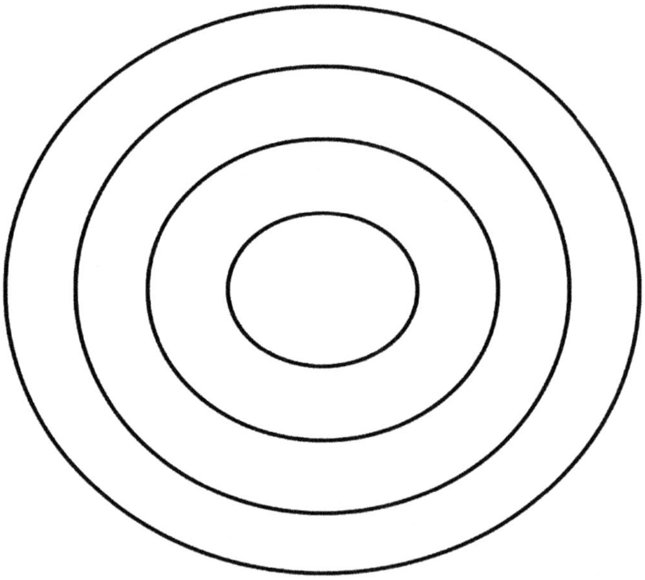

The chart below is for you to use to show how your relationships actually are:

2. Self-evaluate the relationship between your current behavior and your best interests.

13

NEEDS AND RELATIONSHIPS

Although we always strive to meet our five basic needs (LAFFS), in Dynamic Discovery we only evaluate for the first three needs:

1. Love and Belonging
2. Achievement, Power and Recognition
3. Freedom

The fourth need is Fun, which is generally met when the three primary needs are in balance.

The fifth need is Survival, and by merely showing up, you acknowledge that.

When self-evaluating the ways that you use to meet your needs, you can determine whether it is the activity or the people, or both, that is need-fulfilling.

You can use an activity or relationship to meet more than one need, and you can evaluate how to meet your needs to a greater extent. That puts you in control of how much quality you have in your life and how to get it.

When a relationship fails to meet your needs, you may find upon evaluation that a selection error has occurred or that the relationship never met one of your basic needs – maybe it was a relationship based upon guilt or dependency or enabling, rather than being based upon a 'need' connection.

KEY QUESTIONS

1. What do you think you have been doing to get your needs met?

____

____

____

____

2. What needs are being met by your relationships?

____

____

____

3. What could you do instead to meet your needs?

____

____

____

ACTIVITIES

1. Draw out your Needs Circle to chart behaviors and relationships which satisfy your basic needs. The chart below is from one client's 'Ideal World'. The figure below that can be used to draw your actual Needs chart.

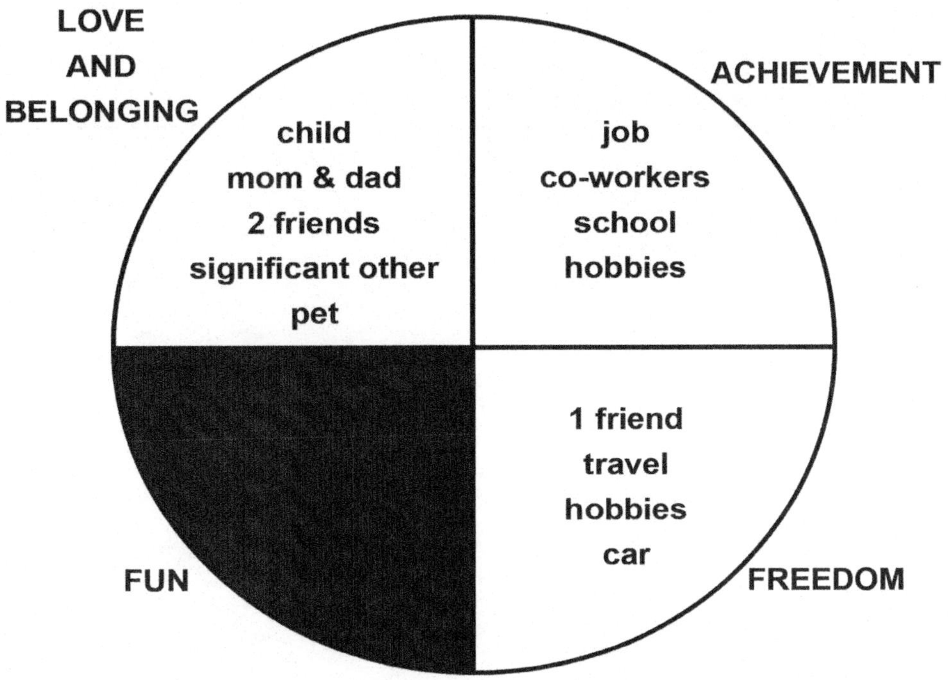

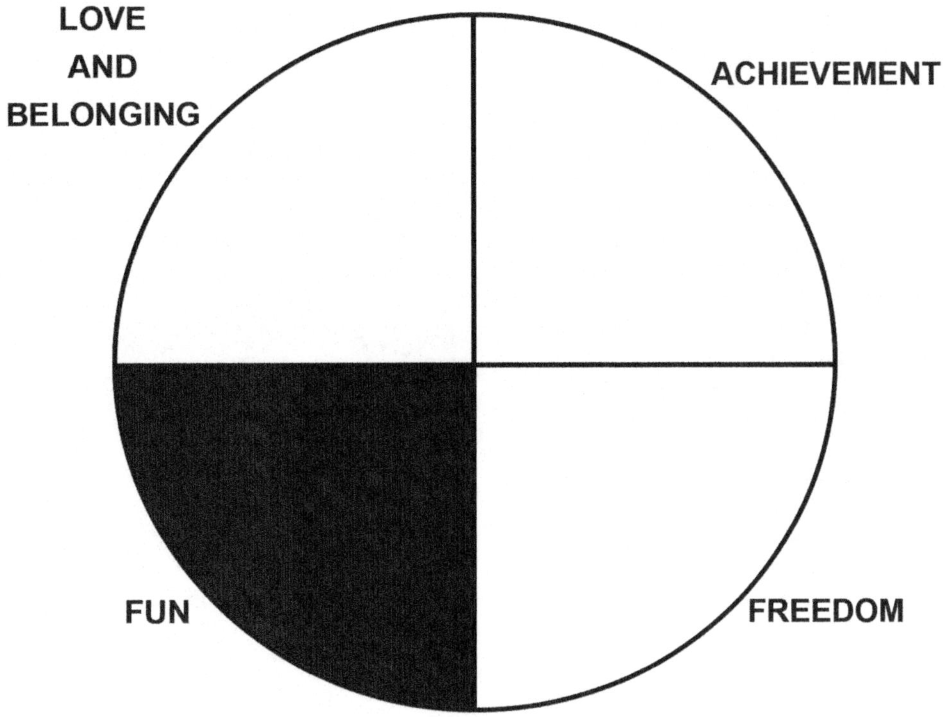

2. Write out ways for you to start to satisfy your unmet needs.

14

FUTURIZE YOUR FANTASY

(Having your world the way you want it to be)

PURPOSE:

To identify the needs you are controlling for. This exercise is not designed to resolve issues – it is designed to start meeting needs.

PLAN:

1. If your world was the way you wanted it five years from now, what would it 'look' like? (Thinking, Doing, Feeling)
2. Writing it out is more effective and hooks into our beliefs.

CRITERIA:

1. Not dependent on anyone else to make it happen.
2. Occurs five years in the future.
3. Takes place on this planet.
4. For general audiences only (not sexually explicit).

The purpose is to identify what needs we are controlling for.

EVALUATION:

1. Look for the energy and the needs being met by your fantasy.
2. The fantasy is a way to get permission to enter the new world being envisioned.
3. What would you be thinking, doing and feeling if your world was exactly the way you wanted it to be?

So how do you work out your fantasy? In an actual Dynamic Discovery workshop, the leader provides a scenario and asks the group some questions:

You go to sleep tonight and something magical happens. All the desired advances in your life have taken place. The magical event happens while you are asleep so you don't actually know that it has happened.

When you wake up in the morning, what is the first thing that you will notice you are doing that will tell you the magical event has happened?

What next?

Each person writes words or draws a picture or series of pictures to represent the differences in their actions. This becomes their Futurized Fantasy.

Now write out your response to the scenario and the questions:

1. When you wake up in the morning, what is the first thing that you will notice you are doing that will tell you the magical event has happened?

____

____

____

2. What next?

____

____

3. Write words or draw a picture or series of pictures to represent the differences in your actions.

____

____

15

DARN GOOD START

This is where we get to start working out solutions and finding ways to start experiencing some victories, and to start building more quality into our lives. Remember, we do not evaluate for right and wrong, or for good and bad. What is is. What ain't ain't. You can't be measured by someone else's yardstick.

CRITERIA:

1. Must be easy to do and not doing now.
2. Must be something we want to do.
3. Must be tangible, reportable and timely (doable within 48 to 72 hrs).
4. Doing it once is rewarding.
5. Continuing to do Darn Good Starts (DGSs) will help meet the need.
6. It must address the need rather than the want.

This is our prescription for meaningful change. Continuous and constant application conditions us to structure winning and control in our lives. We always use LAFFS to determine what we are DGSing for:

1. Are you interested in finding something else to do that will get you what you really want?

(Yes) ___ (No) ___

If you don't know, do a fantasy exercise to find the need(s) you want to satisfy.

2. The action might involve just making a list of things we might like to do and aren't doing now.

3. Define your expectation of a DGS, and what a DGS would look like to you. One way is to ask yourself, "What would I want to be doing if I knew I could not fail?"

____

____

____

4. You must understand and deal with the way things really are.

5. Is it safe? (Yes) ___ (No) ___

Write out your DGS below.

____

____

____

____

16

SOLUTIONS

KEY QUESTIONS

1. Are you interested in finding something else to do that will get you what you really want?

(Yes) ___ (No) ____

If your answer was yes, describe what that 'something else' is:

____

____

2. Is it easily attainable? (Yes) ___ (No) ____

If your answer was yes, describe how you plan to attain it:

____

____

____

3. Is it an action that is reportable?

(Yes) ___ (No) ____

Indicate to whom you will report:

____

____

____

____

____

4. Is it something you want to do?

(Yes) ___ (No) ____

Describe why you want to do it:

____

____

____

5. Will you benefit by doing it once?

(Yes) ___ (No) ____

Describe what benefits you 'see':

____

____

____

6. If you keep doing it, will it meet your needs?

(Yes) ___ (No) ____

Describe how you 'see' it meeting your needs:

____

____

____

ACTIVITIES

1. Evaluate your written fantasy for evidence of unmet needs.

Describe how you 'see' your unmet needs:

2. Planning win-win solutions.

Describe in detail what would constitute a solution – describe it as you 'see' it:

Because I've used the 'magic' question (involving a sudden miraculous solution) in several places within this workbook, I want to explain the reason: We use it because we want people to feel the answer, to experience it, and not just to think about it. This helps to make the imagined future more real and not just a theoretical construct.

Visualizing is a way to get you to 'go inside' for a few moments and really 'see and feel' the question.

With your eyes closed, imagine the following: If, by some very real magic, you were to go to sleep tonight and a miracle happened while you were sleeping, and when you woke in the morning, you and your life was in an altogether happier place, as if the problem has been swept away… just imagine how that would feel. How will it be? What will you do?

Take some time to carry out this visualization exercise and then write out the answers to the following questions:

Describe how it felt:

Describe how it will be:

Describe what you will do:

This exercise will:

- give you a flavour and a 'blueprint' for how things might be different
- give you an idea of how to manage your expectations and develop a strategy for future work.

Sometimes people need a little coaxing to enter into the spirit of 'fantasy' questioning. And sometimes we all need encouragement to see the good things that have already occurred or are happening right now. Using this type of question is a wonderful way to bypass the usual worries about how things could change, and to switch to a motivational focus on what you really want changed.

In hypnotherapy, we use a variation of this approach by first inducing a full state of relaxation, which diverts the client's focus away from the problem. Some 50 years ago, Milton Erickson (a well-regarded psychiatrist and hypnotherapist) presented the original version of the 'magic' question which involved asking his client to look into the future and see themselves as they wanted to be, with problems solved, and then to explain what had happened to cause this change to come about. He sometimes also asked clients to think of a date in the future, then worked backwards, asking them what had happened at various points on the way.

Since Erickson's time, thousands of counselors and therapists have adopted and/or adapted the magic question and used it to take the pressure off their clients so as to allow them to 'free-wheel' their imagination and describe what they were really missing in their lives.

Personally, I propose it as a very specific question: "Suppose that while you are relaxing, a magical event has occurred and the problem that brought you here is solved. However, because you are so relaxed, you don't know that the magical event has already happened. When you return to full awareness, you will notice that some things will be different and those things will make you aware that the magical event has taken place. Before you leave my office, you will be able to begin to tell me what is different about you and your life."

AFTERWORD

Thank you for your interest in Dynamic Discovery.

We would love to hear from you. You can connect with us through our website,

www.dynamicdiscovery.ca

Here are a couple of things for you to remember:

- Whenever I am distressed by external things, I have found that my distress is due to my perception of the thing and not to the thing itself. Through the Dynamic Discovery process, I now know how to suspend my perception so as to properly assess whether the distress is real or imagined.
- Once you adopt an attitude of gratitude, you will soon feel truly secure in yourself – it is then that you can really start experiencing the kind of life you desire.
- Nothing is particularly hard if you are able to divide it into small jobs.

It is important for you to understand that your background is an extremely important part of who you are, but it isn't cast in concrete. You can get over it. It's never too late to have a happy childhood. Every day you have new experiences which tomorrow will be part of your background.

Too many people carry their background around with them as if it's a burden that is keeping them from living the rest of their lives – instead of treating it as a learning experience. You can even break patterns that have gone on for generations.

You have to conquer the demons inside you. Otherwise you will pass them on to your children. The demons are your fearful memories; you have to face them and defeat your fears. All courage and strength must be developed by facing our fearful memories and then transcending them by creating a stronger memory.

Sometimes people use age as a convenient excuse to avoid improving their lives: "I'm too old to start something new"; or, "I couldn't learn that at my age".

Other people, though, go on to achieve their greatest accomplishments in life in later years.

It's not important how old you are; what is important is how you think, how you feel, and what you do. Feelings lead to attitudes, attitudes become beliefs, and beliefs become the basis for actions – no matter what your age. Thoughts lead to purposes; purposes go forth in action; actions form habits; habits decide character; and character fixes our destiny. Just adjust your thinking and your age will keep pace.

WHAT IF ALL YOUR PROBLEMS ARE JUST MEMORIES?

Think of a problem that you used to believe you had. If you are having a hard time accepting that the problem is behind you, include every moment that has passed as part of the past. Think of the past as anything that is not happening right now and you can see what choices are available to you with clearer eyes.

Because this is a big change in our thinking, it requires conscious effort to make it a familiar response. Repetition is how we learn. If we're no longer tied to the mistakes of our past, we're free to make decisions based on reason and we'll always be centered enough to respond rather than react. This approach teaches us to remember how we used to behave in a certain way, so that we can finally let go of behaving that way out of habit.

It may sound bizarre, but it works. And it's enlightening. So many of the things we used to believe about ourselves don't have to hold true anymore – not if we don't want them to. So that voice in your head that used to say, "I always pick the wrong direction," or "I'm always late for important stuff," doesn't need to be true right now. That can be the old story.

That was then, this is now; that's the root of this new way of thinking that challenges us to take responsibility by seeing that we actually create our problems by expecting them. If we believe that we have a problem, then we focus on whatever validates that belief.

I have personally found that my life is much, much better and I am much happier when I am grateful – when I develop an attitude of gratitude. In fact, it's one of the most powerful feelings I have ever had.

However, I'm not grateful for the things I own, like my car or my clothing. I'm not grateful for my toys. I do, for the most part, enjoy them, but I'm not grateful for them – because in a flash, they could be taken away... just like all the people who have lost all their possessions (and friends and family) in tragedies like natural disasters or by the acts of people filled with hatred and rage.

For my happiness to be attached to possessions sets me up to be unhappy way too easily. An attitude of gratitude is why many people who have experienced great setbacks have been able to quickly turn in the right direction and start again, just as determined and certain of success as before... because they are grateful for what they DO have.

As for me, what I am grateful for is the knowledge, ability and willingness to learn even more. I am also thankful for the opportunities to use my knowledge and experience so that I can give what I have learned to others.

In addition, I am thankful for my past and current challenges, which have taught and will continue to teach me and strengthen me so that I can overcome and triumph over adversity in the future.

You see, it is these things for which I AM grateful that make everything else in my life work. If I lose my possessions, I can get them all back and more because I have an attitude of gratitude ... at least I have it most of the time.

And what I am most grateful for is the love I share with those close to me and the regard and acceptance I share and receive from people in all walks of life whom I meet socially and through work – many of whom have become friends.

When a person thinks about the people, things, and experiences that they're grateful for, their awareness of the good in their life increases and they start to feel good. What you focus on increases and you have even more to be grateful for.

If enough of us can be gratefully aware of the ways in which we can help each other in times of trouble, more and more people will be helped to work through the inevitable stressful hazards that confront us all.

It is remarkable to see the power that ordinary people have to adapt to reality, however unpleasant. They have a great deal more strength than we often give them credit for. Unassisted in a time of crisis, this strength may fail them – but if we recognize it and build it up, we can help each other through times of trouble.

Ask yourself: is what you're practicing today about where you've been, or where you want to be? Practice feeling how you'll feel and practice doing what you'll do when you get where you're going. Today is practice for tomorrow.

If you really like adventures, here's an interesting affirmation to try on for size: "I am willing that my present and future be totally unlike my past." Willingness is the key.

Finally, consider this: You are the spearhead of evolution. Think about it – you've survived for long enough on this planet to be reading this piece, which means you are extraordinarily super. In fact, you come from a long line of ancestors who managed to survive and have kids, too! All the lessons of those countless years of evolution have been encoded in your brilliant neurology.

You are so much more than you think you are, so you can allow your idea of yourself to begin to open up. You might even become curious about just how much more is possible for you than you previously thought. How much more love, joy, happiness, freedom, fulfillment, leisure time, fun and adventure is possible?

Fill your boots! You are the spearhead of evolution.

REMEMBER THIS...

For those of you who are really 'stuck' because of your 'limiting' Values and Beliefs, you will find a free downloadable workbook (What Are Your Values?) on our website (www.DynamicDiscovery.ca) that was specially devised to provide a concise, systematic way to change those Values and Beliefs that are interfering with your ability to be happy.

TYPICAL WORDS FOR THE EXERCISES

(Recorded from actual group sessions)

HAVE YOU EVER HAD A FEELING YOU DIDN'T LIKE? (AT ANY TIME IN YOUR LIFE)

Anger	Anxious	Apart from
Dependent	Depressed	Different
Discontent	Failure	Frustrated
FEAR (a distressing emotion aroused by impending danger, evil or pain.)		
Hate	Hopeless	Impotent
Inadequate	Incapable	Incompetent
Incomplete	Isolated	Insulted
Lonely	Not desired	Numb
Out of control	Pain	Revengeful
Sad	Separated	Slighted
Spiteful	Tense	Ugly
Unattractive	Uncomfortable	Unhealthy
Unimportant	Unloved	Unhappy
Uninteresting	Unintelligent (stupid)	Different
Uninvolved	Unsuccessful	Unvalued
Unwanted	Useless	Weak

WHAT WOULD YOU SOONER BE FEELING?

Accessible	Adequate	Attractive	Calm	Capable
Comfortable	Complete	Content	Desired	Handsome
Happy	Healthy	Honest	Important	In control
Independent	Involved	Intelligent (smart)	Interested (ing)	Loved (ing)
Part of	Peaceful	Powerful	Respected	Sexy
Strong	Successful	Valued	Wanted	

HAVE YOU EVER HAD A THOUGHT YOU DIDN'T LIKE? (AT ANY TIME IN YOUR LIFE)

Confused

HIDDEN RULES (What were the do's and don'ts ?)

shoulds/shouldn'ts

can't do

could have done

musts/must nots

NICKNAMES (What did you call yourself?)

Spin dryer

HOW WOULD YOU SOONER BE THINKING?

Calm	Compassionate	Dependable
Fun	Kind	Loving
Strong		

HAVE YOU EVER DONE SOMETHING YOU DIDN'T LIKE? (AT ANY TIME IN YOUR LIFE)

Abuse	Arguing	Blaming	Cheating	Crying	Depressing
Drinking	Drugging	Gossiping	Lying	Spying	Revenging
Self-pitying	Sexing	Shout	Sicking	Swearing	Violence
Yelling					

WHAT WOULD YOU SOONER BE DOING?

Accepting	Assertive	Attractive	Caring	Compassionate
Confident	Exercising	Honest	Loving	Open Minded
Peaceful	Sharing	Smart	Spiritual	Strong
Trusting	Volunteering			

TYPICAL QUESTIONS FOR THE EXERCISES

INTRODUCTIONS

1. What has been going on that led you here?
2. What have you done to try to resolve your problems?
3. How did it work out? Did it help you get what you want?
4. What do you want?
5. If you got that, what would it mean to you?

FEELINGS

6. What feelings have you had in your life that you didn't like?
7. How many hours a day are you dealing with feelings you don't like?
8. Which of the feelings on our list have you not felt?
9. Are your feelings the biggest problem you have?
10. How would you like to be feeling?

THINKING

11. What have you been thinking that you don't like? Or, has not helped you get what you want?
12. Have you ever thought you were stupid, a failure, etc., after something you've done?
13. If this is what you are thinking, how would you expect to feel?

14. If you were happy, what would you be thinking?
15. What could you do to start thinking that way?

DOING (ACTIONS)

16. What have you been doing that you do not like doing? Or has not helped you get what you want?
17. Which of the actions on the list have you not done?
18. What do you want to be doing?

PHYSIOLOGY

19. In what ways have activities that you haven't liked doing affected your physiology?
20. How would your life look if things were the way you wanted?
21. What is something you can do to help you get what you want?

BEHAVIOR AND RELATIONSHIPS

22. How has your behavior affected your relationships?
23. What are your best interests, and where are you in relation to them?

NEEDS CIRCLES

24. What do you think you have been doing to get your needs met?
25. What needs are being met by your relationships?
26. What could you do instead to meet your needs?

SOLUTIONS (WIN-WIN)

27. Are you interested in finding something else to do that will get you what you really want?
28. Is it easily attainable?
29. Is it an action that is reportable?
30. Is it something you want to do?
31. Will you benefit by doing it once?
32. If you keep doing it, will it meet your needs?

RESOURCES

Adult Children of Alcoholics, Janet Geringer Woititz

The Adventures of Anybody, Richard Bandler

Alcoholics Anonymous, Alcoholics Anonymous World Services Inc.

Anxiety & Phobia Workbook, Edmond Bourne

Archives of General Psychiatry

The Art of War, Sun Tzu

Big Book of NLP, Shlomo Vaknin

Blueprint For Progress, Alanon Family Groups

Building Emotional Intelligence, Linda Lantieri

Business NLP for Dummies, Lynne Cooper

Change Your Brain Change Your Life, Daniel G. Amen

Change Your Mind And Keep The Change, Steve Andreas & Connierae Andreas

Chickenhawk Back In The World Life After Vietnam, Robert Mason

Clinicians Brain Science Toolbox, Daniel G. Amen

Codependents Guide to The Twelve Steps, Melody Beattie

Codependent No More, Melody Beattie

Codependent No More Workbook, Melody Beattie

The Complete ACOA Sourcebook, Janet Geringer Woititz

Core Transformation, Connirae Andreas and Tamara Andreas

The Courage To Heal Workbook, Laura Davis

Daybreak Meditations For Women Survivors of Sexual Abuse, Hazeldon Meditations

Dynamic Discovery, George Bissett

Dynamic Discovery Workbook, George Bissett (and many other books)

Frogs into Princes, Richard Bandler and John Grinder (live)

From Survival To Recovery, Alanon

Giving Your Kids The Gift of Inner Discipline, Barbara Coloroso

Healing ADD, Daniel Amen (both editions)

The Healing ADD Power Program, Daniel G. Amen

Healing In Hypnosis, Milton H. Erickson

Healing The Child Within, Charles Whitfield

Healing Trauma, Peter A. Levine

Healing In Hypnosis, Milton H. Erickson

Heart of the Mind, Connirae Andreas and Steve Andreas

How Alanon Works, Alanon Family Groups

Hypnotherapy, Dave Elman

Handbook of Hypnotic Suggestions & Metaphors, Hammond D. Corydon

The Intimacy Struggle, Janet Geringer Woititz

It Will Never Happen To Me, Claudia Black

Kids Are Worth IT, Barbara Coloroso

The Language of Letting Go, Melody Beattie (many other books)

Lifeskills for Adult Children, Janet Geringer Woititz

Lincoln The Unknown, Dale Carnegie

Magnificent Mind At Any Age, Daniel G. Amen

Matrix Energetics, Richard Bartlett

Neuro Linguistic Programming Workbook for Dummies, Ready & Burton

NLP Workbook, Joseph O'Connor

The Physics Of Miracles, Richard Bartlett

Preventing Alzheimer's, William Rodman Shankle and Daniel G. Amen

Parenting Through Crisis: Helping Kids In Times of Loss, Grief, And Change, Barbara Coloroso

Recovering From The War, Patience Mason

Releasing PTSD: The Client Session (program), Steve Andreas

Richard Bandler's Guide to Trans-formation, How To Harness The Power of Hypnosis To Ignite Effortless and Lasting Change, Richard Bandler

Self Hypnosis for Dummies, Bryant & Mabbutt

The Structure of Magic, Richard Bandler & John Grinder

The Structure of Magic II, Richard Bandler & John Grinder

Struggle for Intimacy, Janet Geringer Woititz

Superself, Charles J. Givens

The Teachings of Don Juan: A Yaqui Way of Knowledge, Carlos Castanada (and many other books)

Theraputic Metaphors, David Gordon

Trans-formations: Neuro Linguistic Programming & The Structure of Hypnosis, John

Grinder

Twelve Steps Twelve Traditions, Alcoholics Anonymous World Services

Unchain Your Brain (10 steps to breaking the addictions that steal your life), Daniel G. Amen

Working With Emotional Intelligence, Daniel Goldman

OTHER BOOKS BY BOB BRAY & GEORGE BISSETT

PTSD Road to Recovery: One Soldiers Story

PTSD Road to Recovery Workbook

Trauma and Recovery Guide for victims of Sexual Abuse

Codependency

How to Control Stress

Your Destiny In Motion

Blaming

Overcoming Fear

Alcohol Recovery Guide

Printed in Dunstable, United Kingdom

91219591R00092